The Dementia Caregivers
Bible

**Ultimate strategies, stories, and scriptures
to improve communication, manage behavior, and avoid burnout,
lessening the rigorous impact of the journey**

By Kara L. Kent

B.S.R., M.A.M.C., C.P.L.C.
Chaplain, Certified Professional Life Coach, Dementia Caregiver

Book Cover by 99Designs

Illustrations by Midjourney

1st edition 2024

FOREWORD

This is fantastic work Kara has created! As an ObGyn physician of 40 years, medical director for 16 years, and caregiver for my dear wife of 56 years for 5 years, as well as a practicing Catholic Christian, I can say that this wonderful book about dementia is a must-read for any dementia caregiver.

Over the last five years I have struggled to learn how to be a good caregiver to my wife with Alzheimer's Disease. Nothing in medical school prepared me for this journey even though in the beginning I would be well suited for this adventure. Being a caregiver for dementia patients is an all-consuming task which challenges even the strongest and can bring us to our knees literally and figuratively.

As a physician, I knew the scientific issues and the facts, but I didn't realize that I, too, was helpless in changing the outcome of this disease. I desperately needed the help outlined in this book. Some of it I got from books, fellow caregivers, therapists, and priests, and some I just got with on-the-job training.

What I love about The Dementia Caregivers Bible is that it includes the spiritual aspect of this disease and the need for the caregiver to rely on God or some higher power to help them through the rigors of this long process.

Scripture tells us that "God is Love" and that we are to love God with our whole heart, mind, and strength and to love our neighbor as ourselves. So as a caregiver we are to love our dementia spouse or patient as we love God. What does that mean? If we define "Love as willing the good of the other" just like God does, we are charged with loving our DP in every aspect of their disease journey. In this book, Kara does a wonderful job of telling us just how to do that loving.

God Bless all you caregivers.

- John W. Knispel BS, MD, FACOG, CPE

What happens when dementia is diagnosed? Kara takes us on an authentic journey of wisely addressing the path when one is called upon to be a caregiver. She combines beneficial therapeutic, practical, and scientific approaches while holding forth hope, which her Christian faith provides, for being a patient, effective caregiver.

This material offers a comprehensive view that addresses the many complex issues that dementia creates. Above all, here is an encompassing reference manual for anyone who is called upon to serve others with this condition. "The Dementia Caregivers Bible" is a much-needed book at a time when this issue is expanding daily and at the center of our national conversation.

As a Care Pastor, this is an excellent tool that will be prominent on my desk as a ready resource for those seeking guidance and truth in this area.

- Rev. George D. Ray,
Care Pastor, Calvary Church, Jupiter, Florida
BA, JD, MDiv

CONTENTS

PART II

INTRODUCTION

A massive rainstorm propelled us together on the west side track & field of Deer Run High in 1965. That electrified moment we met remains etched in memory as vividly as the crackling of thunder and lightning that forced us beneath the shelter of the wooden bleachers. What could have been a dreadful encounter with the elements transformed into the inception of a beautiful life together. Even though he was a senior and I was a sophomore, our conversation flowed effortlessly from the outset, revealing an abundance of shared interests that ignited a spark within us both. As the rain tapped its rhythm above, we delved into the stories of our preferences, from the mundane to the profound. It was remarkable how our affinities aligned – the same sports teams, favorite movies, foods, and places. We didn't seem to notice how sopping wet or shivering cold we were; we only noticed that something special was happening. Inevitably, our affection for each other blossomed in that serendipitous moment and has lasted some 52 years.

Over these years, we've amassed a treasure trove of memories – a tapestry woven with threads of love, joy, sorrow, and perseverance. These shared experiences and our deep spiritual commitment serve as a solid anchor that binds us together, securing us through life's ebbs and flows, highs and lows. In times when familiarity is vague, our commonalities serve as lanterns, illuminating the path back to each other as we search for God's perfect will. They serve as portals to cherished recollections, unlocked by the melodies of music, the nostalgia of movies, favorite books, the warmth of shared stories, familiar aromas, the presence of dear friends, and the embrace of mutual biblical beliefs.

Some may speak of dementia as a thief, gradually pilfering memories until only shadows remain. Yet, it merely overlays them with tenacious layers of forgetfulness. Like a masterpiece hidden beneath coats of ugly paint, our shared history remains intact underneath, though it's become a secret to one of us. Though the passage of time may obscure moments once cherished, fragments of our past occasionally emerge like a chip off a veneer, offering glimpses of the beauty or agony that we've shared. These fleeting reminders are a testament to the enduring bond that unites us, transcending the cruelty of dementia. In these memories and commitments, we caregivers move dutifully forward. As a spouse, it is a love based on "until death does us part." Or, as an adult child, it is as if *we* become the caring parent, and as a respite family member, friend, or professional, it is for compassionate, altruistic service.

The goal and purpose of this book is to offer you a daily dose of hope, well-tested tools, and ideas to utilize as a caregiver while you're on this unwelcome journey. I, Kara, call this book a *Bible* to indicate that it's a trustworthy go-to source to deal with life's problems, pain, and even pleasures along the way. It is to be read in tandem with doctors' and nurses' orders, not in place of. This includes an arsenal of critically important information plus biblical strength-building promises that hold courage, comfort, and divine direction. In these pages, you'll find helpful ideas and support for your soul, supplements of courage and peace to sustain you through the upcoming days. You are not alone; you are part of a group of unsung heroes to your loved ones with dementia and to so many who know how much you care with all the ways you show it. C.S. Lewis writes in The Problem of Pain, "Pain provides an opportunity for heroism; the opportunity is seized with surprising frequency." (Lewis, 1948, p.145)

I will use the umbrella term dementia in this book as it can refer to all kinds of dementias with varying degrees of symptoms and causes. Every dementia has no absolute cure, in the natural world. Nevertheless, we must know that God is able to heal supernaturally if He intends to, and if we fast and pray in faith for this, as it is written; "This kind does not go out except by prayer and fasting." Matthew 17:21 Though healing is always God's will, He may have other eternal plans in place as well and they may include developing the caregiver. That is why the main focus of this book is you, the caregiver. I, the author, endeavor to guide and support you, as you deliver general treatments, practical, compassionate care, and plenty of common sense for the benefit of your person or patient with dementia (DP). Since doing this is physically, emotionally, and spiritually depleting over time, I offer ways to maintain your health and sanity, even sharpen and improve them for the duration. It's been said by many in ministry that, *God doesn't call the equipped, He equips the called.* If you are the primary caregiver, you will indeed see this in your experience. To illustrate this, I have included several personal stories of mine and other colleagues that offer tips to make this guide unique.

"Come to Me, all you who labor and are heavy laden, and I will give you rest. Take My yoke upon you and learn from Me, for I am gentle and lowly in heart, and you will find rest for your souls. For My yoke is easy and My burden is light." - Matthew 11:28-3.

Under the vast expanse of the human experience, few conditions resonate with the profundity and complexity of dementia of a once vibrant, fully capable person. These dementia disorders are shrouded in misconceptions and have many challenges. Dementia's intellectual and personality demise is gradual, sometimes almost imperceptible. The path of a caregiver is strewn with both tangible and intangible hurdles, demanding not only a profound reservoir of patience and stamina but also a good amount of ingenuity. It is here, at the confluence of love and duty, where our journey into the heart of dementia caregiving begins.

"Remember, dear brothers and sisters, that few of you were wise in the world's eyes or powerful or wealthy when God called you. Instead, God chose things the world considers foolish in order to shame those who think they are wise. And he chose things that are powerless to shame those who are powerful."- I Corinthians 1:26-27.

"And God is able to make all grace abound toward you, that you, always having all sufficiency in all things, may have an abundance for every good work."- II Corinthians 9:8.

Many seniors are caregivers for their spouse or partner, I want to say, 'I see you'. I understand the emotional stages you're facing, the fears, challenges, and the love that drives you. Adult children, family members or close friends all go through the same or similar emotional stages as well. Rest assured that what you do not only makes an enormous difference for the DP, but it will also have eternal ramifications of joyful rewards. This book will be a faithful companion on the sometimes-rocky caregiving path. These pages contain resources you can turn to time and again for comfort, guidance and information. When one is in emotional or physical pain, it becomes acutely necessary to continually feed oneself with rich, hopeful truths and positive biblical words to meditate on daily. This can be as important as medical advice and medications. Spiritual sustenance can bring about courage and peace amidst trouble and fear. This area is too often neglected and costs far too high a price for both the caregiver and the DP.

"Because he has set his love upon Me, therefore I will deliver him; I will set him on high, because he has known My name. He shall call upon Me, and I will answer him; I will be with him in trouble; I will deliver him and honor him. With long life I will satisfy him and show him My salvation." - Psalm 91:14-16.

Welcome to a journey of hope, hardship, and the heart's capacity to love through it all. I hope that as you turn these pages, you'll find the motivation and peace you will need to navigate this challenging path, knowing when it's time to rest and recuperate.

"Be still and know that I am God;" - Psalm 46:10.

"Ah Lord God! You made the heavens and the earth by your strong hand and powerful arm. Nothing is too difficult for you!" - Jeremiah 32:17

"Thus says the Lord to you: 'Do not be afraid nor dismayed because of this great multitude, for the battle is not yours, but God's.'" - II Chronicles 20:15.

PART I

1

DECODING DEMENTIA: A COMPASSIONATE OVERVIEW

D ementia is an umbrella term for loss of memory and various thinking abilities that interfere with one's daily life routines. "Dementia is the name for a group of symptoms that make it hard to remember, think clearly, make decisions, or even control your emotions and outbursts. There are four known main types of dementia listed in order of occurrence: Alzheimer's, Vascular, Lewy Body, and Frontotemporal. Alzheimer's was named after Dr. Alois Alzheimer in 1906. It is a neurodegenerative disease that is the most common cause of dementia. Dementia describes a wide range of symptoms, including this disease." These symptoms impact a person's ability to perform everyday activities independently, interfering with short-term and long-term memories. (Alzheimer's Association)

Scientists believe that Alzheimer's disease is caused by a toxic amyloid-beta protein build-up in the brain, causing tangled nerves. A full clinical workup is still necessary; as with any biomarker, simply detecting biological changes is insufficient for definitive diagnosis. In Alzheimer's, the brain may show signs of the disease before the person experiences any outward symptoms, 5, 10, or even 20 years before they appear. The build-up takes time, so the evidence of damage is also gradual. Symptoms usually start with difficulty remembering new information. The complete list of early warning signs can be found at www.alz.org." (Alzheimer's Association)

"Alzheimer's accounts for 60% to 80% of dementia cases." Approximately 5.7 million people in the U.S. currently have Alzheimer's disease. The number of Americans with Alzheimer's is projected to triple to 16 million by 2050. Someone in the United States develops Alzheimer's every 65 seconds. By 2050, this is projected to be every 33 seconds. Alzheimer's is not just a disease of old age: 200,000 people under age 65 have an early-onset diagnosis. "Worldwide, about 50 million people have some form of dementia, and someone in the world develops dementia every three seconds. Alzheimer's is the most common form of dementia, a progressive brain disease that slowly destroys memories and thinking skills. In advanced stages, symptoms include confusion, mood and behavior changes, and inability to care for oneself and perform basic life tasks. Alzheimer's is ultimately fatal. It is currently the sixth-place cause of death in the US. (National Institute on Aging) The disease takes the lives of an estimated 500,000 Americans every year." "It is the only top-10 cause of death in the United States with no known cure. Alzheimer's disproportionately impacts women and people of color." (World Health Organization)

"I am the Alpha and the Omega, the Beginning and the End, the First and the Last." - Revelation 22:13

1.2. It takes courage to seek a doctor's opinion about one's lessening cognitive abilities. It is these early whispers of the condition that may cause concern. If the problem grows beyond benign age-appropriate forgetfulness, it might just be time to seek the truth. Misconceptions abound, with many quick to attribute memory lapses to aging rather than the onset of dementia. However, a comprehensive assessment by a healthcare professional can delineate between normal aging and the early stages of dementia, setting the stage for informed caregiving strategies and even some interventions. It can relieve anxiety by knowing what lies ahead, whatever the diagnosis. Since this information-seeking step at the doctor's office can be stressful, I recommend that you (or all of you) gather a fortified stance that no matter what you hear at this first appointment, you will trust God to get you through it and seek His peace and direction as you traverse this unknown territory together.

In this area of uncertainty, where fear and hope mingle, the role of faith becomes paramount. Faith is the essential ingredient for interacting with God, for it is impossible to please Him without faith (Hebrews 11:6). Call upon God every day for strength and help. As we stand on the precipice of the unknown, these words offer solace and divine help.

"From the ends of the earth, I will cry to You, when my heart is overwhelmed; lead me to the rock that is higher than I." - Psalm 61:2

"Likewise, the Spirit also helps with our weaknesses. For we do not know what we should pray for as we ought, but the Spirit Himself makes intercession for us with groanings which cannot be uttered." - Romans 8:26.

1.3. Early detection can impact the management of dementia by having the time to get prepared. It is important to address all current health matters now when the DP can tell you what they're feeling. A full physical for a benchmark is beneficial to know their overall physical condition. If you wait until certain symptoms are unmanageable, putting the suggested strategies in place becomes an uphill climb, though it can be done. Evaluate and correct any vitamin and mineral deficiencies, if possible. Get new eyesight and hearing assessments now while they can respond to the prompts. Read about the possibility of delaying the progression of symptoms online or in these books, "The End of Alzheimer's" by Dr. Dale Bredesen and "The Alzheimer's Solution", by Drs. Dean and Ayesha Sherzai. Though there is no known cure for the disease, lifestyle changes can benefit most anyone diagnosed, if the diagnosis is determined early.

Once medically diagnosed, whether you share this personal data with anyone other than close family members is fraught with potential misunderstanding and even the intimacy of people who were once in your inner circle. If the condition is Alzheimer's, it may be wise to explain the problem as dementia rather than the emotionally charged term Alzheimer's. The term dementia is still the truth, it's just a little more placid. Friends separating from the DP is usually a knee-jerk reaction based on ignorance upon hearing terms like dementia or Alzheimer's. It, unfortunately, frightens some away. More education about the social stigma is needed for these folks. Their best friend will hopefully be you and maybe their beloved pet(s) too. See Chapter 6.

Knowing when to share the news is unique for each family situation. Be sensitive and aware of how your beloved DP feels about it. The last thing you want is to embarrass them or let them feel inferior or that their life is on a fast track to destruction. It may be best to keep your cards close to your chest until dementia introduces itself naturally, reassuring others and teaching your friends what they don't know. However, certain people the DP routinely sees need to know upfront. Communicating this must be done with grace and finesse, especially if the DP is listening. More on this topic can be found in Chapter 9.

Unfortunately, and entirely detrimental, dementia is often accompanied by shame and isolation. It occurs in both the patient and their family members who care for them, as well as friends. It ought not to be so. What other diseases do we tend to shun people? Dementia and specifically Alzheimer's, is burgeoning daily. It is, sadly, common among the Baby Boomer generation as 1 in 10 people over 65 have some form of dementia, primarily Alzheimer's. Its prevalence increases with age. This disease must come out of the shadows and into the light of day and the light of God's mercy and love. There is no shame in dementia, no more than any other disease whatsoever. Stereotypes and prejudice grow in the darkness of ignorance. The fear and sometimes even mocking of dementia patients promote a less acceptable age-related problem. We don't mock people with arthritis or silver hair, we must exhibit grace, honor, and respect for the Silent Generation (1928-1945), Baby Boomers (1946-1964), and Generation X (1965-1980).

Having said that, caregivers can be on the front line in reducing shame and isolation with positive preparation and knowledge. These can provide a semblance of control amidst the chaos, offering caregivers a framework to adapt their approach as dementia progresses. The trajectory from early, mild stages to more advanced stages of dementia is marked not only by the decline in memory and cognitive functions but also by the transformation in the needs and behaviors of those affected. This process necessitates a dynamic caregiving approach, one that evolves in tandem with changing needs. It also necessitates that you rely more on your relationship with the Lord and those friends who stick around, no matter what.

"A man/woman who has friends must themselves be friendly, but there is a friend who sticks closer than a brother." - Proverbs 18:24.

Refer to this list of the stages from the Alzheimer's Association:

Stage 1. Pre-clinical Alzheimer's Disease: This stage may start 5 to 20 years before any noticeable symptoms appear though changes are happening in the brain, such as the accumulation of beta-amyloid protein plaques and tau tangles.

Stage 2. Mild Cognitive Impairment (MCI): In this stage, individuals may experience mild memory problems and cognitive decline beyond what is considered normal for their age. However, the symptoms are not severe enough to significantly interfere with daily functioning or independence. Some people may progress to Alzheimer's disease, while others may remain stable or even improve, thus revealing they do not have the disease.

Stage 3. Early-stage Alzheimer's: This stage typically involves mild to moderate cognitive decline. Symptoms may include:

- Memory lapses, particularly of recent events or newly learned information.
- Difficulty with tasks that require planning, organization, or problem-solving.
- Confusion about time or place.
- Challenges with language, such as finding the right words or following conversations.
- Mood changes, such as increased irritability, anxiety, or depression.
- Withdrawal from social activities or hobbies.
- Difficulty with driving or other complex activities.

Stage 4. Middle or Moderate Stage Alzheimer's: Symptoms become more pronounced and interfere more with daily life. Common behaviors and symptoms include:

- Increased memory loss and confusion, forgetting details about oneself and family members.
- Difficulty recognizing familiar people or places.
- Problems with communication, difficulty following conversations or expressing thoughts.
- Wandering or getting lost, even in familiar surroundings.
- Changes in sleep patterns, such as insomnia or increased daytime napping.
- Agitation, aggression, or other behavioral changes.
- Hallucinations or delusions.
- Increased dependence on others for daily activities such as bathing, dressing, and eating.

Stage 5. Late-stage or Severe Alzheimer's: In the final stage, individuals require round-the-clock care and assistance with all aspects of daily living. Symptoms may include:

- Severe cognitive decline, with little to no awareness of time, place, or people.
- Inability to communicate verbally.
- Difficulty swallowing, leading to weight loss and increased risk of aspiration pneumonia.
- Loss of mobility and ability to control movements.
- Increased susceptibility to infections.
- Loss of bladder and bowel control.
- Seizures, skin infections, and other complications.
- Eventually, individuals become bedridden and require palliative care.

The disease can vary widely among individuals, and not everyone will experience all of these symptoms. People with Alzheimer's disease or some dementias may also experience the progression of other health conditions or complications that can affect their symptoms and behaviors. Thus, their poor behavior is rarely intentional. Alzheimer's is a heart-rending, ever-changing cycle of goodbyes to who they once were and hellos to the next new person.

"Therefore, whoever hears these sayings of Mine, and does them, I will liken him to a wise man who built his house on the rock: and the rain descended, the floods came, and the winds blew and beat on that house; and it did not fall, for it was founded on the rock." - Matthew 7:24-25.

1.4. Once diagnosed with Alzheimer's disease, the **average** life span is in the six-ten years range. Dementia is ancillary to who they genuinely are; it is deceptive to both them and you, especially in the early stage. At the core, your DP is the same person; no matter how different they act or speak, these are just symptoms of an illness. When one has a cold, they cough, sneeze, are extra tired, etc., but they are the same at their core. Of course, a cold is temporary, but the point is that your DP is not the diagnosis; they remain under the symptoms even in the late stages. They cannot untangle the brain's mess to show you. Early on, many DP's vigorously deny that they have it. Please refrain from insisting the truth upon them. Nevertheless, you will see many changes ahead that will eventually, and sadly, convince them.

It is a truth you must be aware of; you, too, will change. If you seek the recommendations in this book, the changes can improve your life physically, spiritually, and emotionally. Their dementia syndrome or Alzheimer's disease diagnosis does not need to damage or destroy you. Please settle this in your heart that dementia, in all its forms, is not from God; it is a natural byproduct of life on earth. Nevertheless, as with all disorders, it is allowed due to the human freedom that we all have, as described in Genesis 3. It is not that anyone chooses a disease, nor has the DP done things to cause it (that are objective facts); it is just a part of the original curse and exists because of this curse. There is no blame, no shame to be aimed; it just simply is. See Chapter 13 for more spiritual assessment. If one-day modern medicine uncovers more details that can prevent or cure it, then we will have some control. But today, there is none known to stop or reverse it. God's power is stronger than the diagnosis, so stand fast in His power and love to serve.

"For I consider that the sufferings of this present time are not worthy to be compared with the glory which shall be revealed in us." - Romans 8:18.

"But we have this treasure in earthen vessels, that the excellence of the power may be of God and not of us. We are hard-pressed on every side, yet not crushed; we are perplexed, but not in despair; persecuted, but not forsaken; struck down, but not destroyed— always carrying about in the body the dying of the Lord Jesus, that the life of Jesus may also be manifested in our body." - II Corinthians 4:7-10.

1.5. Biblical Spirituality plays a paramount role in accepting the diagnosis with grace and courage. It is possible to minimize the feelings of shock, anxiousness, and anger through acceptance. Erma Bombeck once said, "Worry is like a rocking chair, it gives me something to do but gets me nowhere." This is the time to get ready and deny worry it's pull through a deepening reliance on your spiritual life. After all, wise followers know Who the ultimate power is and how to garner solutions for living life in a peace-filled way instead of the more common short-sighted, ineffective way. Acceptance is the first answer. This involves a deep internal process of embracing reality as it is, without resistance or denial. It also consists of living in the present moment, embracing the imperfect nature of this journey, and recognizing that problems are a natural part of the process and do not diminish one's worth or potential for growth. Acceptance is about self-compassion for being imperfect and knowing the importance of surrendering to God, who is perfect.

"Be anxious for nothing, but in everything by prayer and supplication, with thanksgiving, let your requests be made known to God and the peace of God which transcends all understanding will guard your hearts and minds in Christ Jesus." - Philippians 4:6-7

1.6. Face the harsh truth: denial will not prevent the inevitable; it will only complicate the future because of an unwillingness to get prepared. Your DP may deal with some denial as it is so hard for them to face *senility*. Nevertheless, it is paramount to keep on the high road of emotional and spiritual health as the days of fatigue and fear will likely come soon enough. A solid knowledge of and dependence on God and His love is essential in keeping you, the caregiver grounded during trying times. The high road must be approached in tandem with a much higher power, God. He reaches down to take your wrist, not your hand, as a hand can too easily slip away. Visualize this wrist-to-wrist position, it is stronger and more secure. It is of utmost importance to recognize the hold God has on you and in you and how very much you depend on Him. If your hand slips, He's still got you. It is not to be sought with the natural mind, it is supernatural and powerful. This does not mean you set aside your wisdom or practical skills, these too are from the Creator and are critically needed.

To step into the role of a caregiver with dementia is to answer a sacred call—a call that requires a heart fortified by faith and a spirit resilient in the face of trials. This calling is not for the faint of heart, nor is it a path walked in isolation. This profound connection infuses each action and each decision with a sense of divine purpose, transforming the act of caregiving into a service that transcends the mundane and elevates it to a spiritual ministry. To fill your faith tank, think about these:

"So then faith comes by hearing, and hearing by the word of God." - Romans 10:17

"The LORD himself goes before you and will be with you; he will never leave you nor forsake you. Do not be afraid; do not be discouraged." - Deuteronomy 31:8

"For I know the plans I have for you, declares the Lord, plans to prosper you and not to harm you, plans to give you hope and a future." - Jeremiah 29:11.

2

DIRECTING THE STEPS IN THE DEMENTIA DILEMMA

This navigation requires a multifaceted approach that balances the management of symptoms with the preservation of the individual's self-worth and quality of life. As caregivers, our arsenal must be equipped with both a little personal medical knowledge and a lot of compassionate strategies and tools, allowing us to adapt to the fluid needs of those we care for. Arm yourself with realistic expectations and a flexible game plan for each stage of the journey. As this disease usually progresses slowly, if you have the space now, it is wise to begin preparation to improve both your lives with the right home equipment that is handy when you need it. Setting up some of this early may alleviate stress in the future, but before you buy any expensive item that private insurance or Medicare won't cover, realize that your DP may not be able to stay at home for the duration. Each situation is somewhat unique. When you get to that point, most of these items are already provided at a trusted facility.

I found that organizing medical facts and keeping as much practical data in separate folders, notebooks, or on an electronic device is a smart way to preserve knowledge, dates, appointments, and resources to refer to. I also suggest a hard or digital copy of another notebook of respite people, caregiver group contacts, social worker(s), physicians, pharmacists, and anyone on your caregiving team. After seeking your private insurance or Medicare Part B plan coverage for specific items, list places and people where you can purchase, barter, or get for free the things you may need as the DP declines. If your DP is a military veteran, VA benefits may offer dementia patients the necessary equipment and supplies. Include these items on your list and whatever the Physical Therapist or Dr. orders: incontinence materials, a walker, a wheelchair, a bedside toilet, a shower chair, an adjustable bed, bed rails, oxygen pumps, tanks, etc. Most towns have medical supply stores and hospice resale shops with quality pre-owned products to save money. Also, look for a local Dementia and/or Alzheimer's non-profit group. Otherwise, some items can be found at **OfferUp, Facebook Marketplace, eBay,** and **FreeCycle;** type in the zip code and radius for local searches. This search and acquiring task should be for a family member, good friend, or other volunteer to take on, as it is not always as easy as one may think, and you are already preoccupied with your DP's care.

Caregiving needs will evolve as dementia progresses, and new strategies to adapt to these changes for both the DP and caregiver will help you step into the next territory. The fact that you're reading this book shows you endeavor to be aware of ways to begin preparation, seeking options for the middle and latter stages. Acknowledging the reality of the diagnosis is the initial step toward preparation for the journey ahead—a journey that, while demanding, is punctuated with moments of profound beauty and deepening faith. Amid the storm, we are reminded of our reliance on a Power greater than ourselves, a source of unfailing strength and comfort. Remind yourself that it will not all be bad, and by faith, you will know what to do when it is.

"Blessed be the God and Father of our Lord Jesus Christ, the Father of mercies and God of all comfort, who comforts us in all our tribulation, that we may be able to comfort those who are in any trouble, with the comfort with which we ourselves are comforted by God." - I Corinthians 1:3-4.

"He has shown you oh man, what is good. And what does the Lord require of you? But to do justice, to love mercy and to walk humbly with your God." - Micah 6:8

2.2. Important tips to prevent problems in the future, such as attaining the DP's passwords, email and computer logins, PINs, keys, codes, etc., early on, if possible, even if the caregiver knows some of them now. You'll need their friends' names and numbers. Identify and secure the locations for important documents. It is the time to ask them sincere and important questions and get mostly lucid answers. If they are suspicious of your motive, try again another day. Assumptions are not wise; be direct and ask a lot of questions, but not all at once, which may overwhelm them. Even though it is early, now is the time to make sure their final directions and plans are known and documented. You will need to refer to these advanced directives at the last stage of dementia. The power-of-attorney for every financial, medical, legal, etc., decision must be set up before symptoms eradicate the DP's clear thinking. See Chapters 23-24. All preemptive steps will make the more strenuous days less chaotic for you.

Have their vision and hearing checked annually. If these areas decline, it can exaggerate dementia symptoms. If they are used to putting in contact lenses, it will soon be time to switch to glasses, at least two pairs. If they have poor hearing, ensure they have well-fitting, effective hearing aids. Be responsible to keep them in a secure place so they are not lost, though some insurance against loss is wise to procure. It is difficult enough to have memory decline, coupled with age-related decline, can be additionally frustrating. Hearing and seeing well avoids depriving their brain of much-needed data that newer glasses and hearing aids supply and thus lessen their confusion.

"For everything, there is a season, a time for every purpose under heaven." - Ecclesiastes 3:1

"Therefore humble yourselves under the mighty hand of God, that He may exalt you in due time, casting all your care upon Him, for He cares for you." - I Peter 5:6-7

2.3. Here, we'll discuss strategies for communicating with compassion to aid connection. Creative ways to meet the DP's needs and wants without necessarily using words. Some DPs like affectionate hugs or handholding, while others may want to get far away from you or the respite caregiver, but in a few minutes, they may want to cuddle. Many DPs get clingy and want to stay close to you as they sense their memory and abilities are full of holes. Understand this conduct is for their security and comfort. Early on, the DP has enough understanding to know they are slipping away, and they also know that you are their anchor and guide. Realize this and be sensitive to their panic, fear, and caution. Their memory is becoming very unreliable, but you are not. As the days go by, be flexible for today's soup-du-jour, so to speak. What they used to like may now be a bother, so remember not to take it personally. Learn their coping ways, as they still want to communicate with you; it's just going to be different with lots of trial and error. Then, the next month, it may change again, not necessarily getting worse or better, but different. Get used to repetition, both theirs and yours. When you don't want to give the same answer again for the 25th time, change it up and tell a story so it's a bit creative, without guilt. You will soon learn the word "lie" is not so black and white; a fib for the sake of comforting and explaining it to your loved one is merciful. You can protect or calm the DP in many ways, such as by avoiding the cold, hard truth or by softening the pain with a gentler, more creative version. A rule of thought is that there are similarities between communicating with the DP and with a child. Sharing the truth must be done appropriately and cautiously so as not to unnecessarily upset or anger them. A version of the truth can be shared in stories and is often more welcome this way. While on earth, Jesus Himself told many parables to make a point sink in better.

"Then He spoke a parable to them, that men always ought to pray and not lose heart, saying..." - Luke 18:1

"He told them another parable, saying, "The kingdom of heaven is like a grain of mustard seed which a man took and sowed in his field. This indeed is the least of all seeds, but when it has grown, it is the greatest among herbs and is a tree, so that the birds of the air come and lodge in its branches." - Matthew 13:31-32

2.4. Understanding and responding to non-verbal cues as verbal communication declines. "Dementia damages the brain, so the person cannot make sense of what he/she sees and hears." (Mace & Rabins, 2011, p.123) When possible, keep direct eye contact with the DP when talking. Communicating concern, love, value, and many other emotions is crucial. Ideas for non-verbal communication include hand gestures, index cards, or a dry-erase board with pictures of items, activities, places, etc. Keep this at arm level, not eye level, in the kitchen and in the bathroom so they can point to the image. This ability will sometimes come and go, which is typical in the dementia process. If it dissipates one day, do not be surprised to see its return on another day. This is one of those efforts that can be set up early on, certain hand motions may be taught to the DP, but do not expect perfection. Especially a thumbs up or down for yes or no, tapping the tummy for I'm hungry, tapping the lips for I'm thirsty, holding the lower tummy for I've got to use the bathroom, grabbing the shoulders for I'm cold, wiping the forehead for I'm hot, etc. You both can decide the unique way each family chooses to use non-verbal directions. The communication style may need a daily adjustment, as there will be days when it just isn't getting through. A pivot is needed today: try something new, or, better yet, be still and wait for the DP to respond. Occasionally, they may respond in a way you can understand all or part of. During later stages of dementia, these tricks may fall away entirely, so use them when you can, but know they'll have their season. You won't know ahead of time when they quit working; the light of the skill will dim, and it will then simply atrophy. *But God's strength never atrophies.*

"Thy word is a lamp unto my feet and a light unto my path." - Psalm 119:105

"These things I have spoken to you, that in Me you may have peace. In the world you will have tribulation; but be of good cheer, I have overcome the world." - John 16:33

2.5. Tips for creating a positive and reassuring environment that fosters communication. If the DP is your parent, it can be a bit tricky to take care of an aging parent with dementia, even if you have a good relationship with them. If it is not so good, it can become quite a challenge, but not an impossible challenge. This role reversal is strewn with potential upheaval and power struggles. If the DP is early in their disease, they may object to their adult child "bossing" them around. This entire role reversal must be met with extra compassion, tenderness, and respect. It may take time, but it is certainly possible. The situation might repair and strengthen the love for each other as well as add value to the other. It may start with statements like these: "I don't like dementia in your life any more than you do, but I am here for you now." "Let's make the best of this, as I am all-in, for your sake." "Be nice to me; I mean no harm; I'm just here to help you (dad/mom)." "We can have some fun if we can work together; I can do that, can you?" Hopefully, they will, at first, recognize your significant sacrifice and not be resistant to your efforts. Later, the resistance could worsen, but it's only because of dementia's dirty tricks on the brain. Be cautious of developing a martyr's viewpoint; it can cloud your best judgment, and you may even slip into self-pity. If you have a family of your own, be very mindful of your primary commitment to them, and do not take on more than you can. This caregiving role **must** be shared with others, even if you are single and without younger children.

Whether you're an adult child or the DP is your spouse, a friend, or a client, your mood enormously affects them. Everyone can sense the mood of the one who is communicating, so your attitude must be conveyed in gentleness whether the DP understands the words or not. It is extremely important to not let your negative emotions interfere with the directions you give. Employee self-control, and if you're not there, take the time and effort to get there to make it a calm, safe, non-shaming way to communicate. This includes watching out for any angry reactions to what the DP may say or do that is absurd, stubborn, offensive, etc. Remind yourself continually that **it's the disease talking or doing.** Be gentle with yourself, too, and remember good self-care, especially when you are being "accused and tried" for an imaginary offense. Once the issue is gone, they have the benefit of not remembering it at all. For your own well-being, practice the art of ease by choosing forgiveness; just let it go. Holding a grudge is useless and wastes your energy for something good right around the corner. It is never a martyr's call to deny yourself as much love and care as you give your DP. Feeling sorry for your situation must be a fleeting thought; do not camp there; it is a slippery slope downward. Always keep a full cup of compassion on hand for yourself and your DP. These often difficult but great goals to follow are:

"Be kind to one another tenderhearted, forgiving one another, as God in Christ forgave you." - Ephesians 4:32

"If it is possible, as much as depends on you, live peaceably with all men." *"Beloved do not avenge yourselves but rather give place to wrath"* - Romans 12:18-19a

2.6. This section offers techniques for managing real or imagined offenses. When a respite caregiver comes to help, your DP needs to be introduced to the new "friend" over and over whenever possible so they are not alarmed and offended when "a stranger" tries to help them with personal daily activities, like toileting and undressing. A possible scenario is that you and the respite caregiver may sometimes encounter a sharp slap from the DP instead of verbally scolding you. They are reacting to something harmless that they do not understand yet are trying to, to the best of their limited ability. The DP is usually fearful and has miscalculated the motive of the caregiver. Yet physical violence is never the right response; keep in mind that they are not whole mentally, and the rules of respect have been replaced with frustrating aggression. Because words are lost, emotion is often the DP's most common form of communication, so if paranoia, suspicion, or anger comes out too often, investigate and see what they may be feeling and why. Yet if they regularly hit, slap, or push you, a change must be made to keep you safe. Step away and do not try to control them. Let it cool off for a while before trying again, if at all. If they are mostly aggressive with a certain helper, it may be wise to install a hidden camera to see if any roughness, etc., happens on the helper's part. Since the DP may not be able to tell you, it is paramount to keep the DP safe and you informed. It is also a record for the professionals to try to seek a solution for the continuing behavior. There may be nothing wrong at all, but it is best to know for certain.

The DP's forgetfulness of who family and friends will also come. When family/friends are around, they, too, need to be informed of a few dos and don'ts and some nuances of the stages of dementia. Your DP may have the "record player syndrome," like a vinyl record with a scratch that gets stuck and repeats itself incessantly. With repetitive behavior, do not reproduce the behavior yourselves by repeatedly reminding them of their memory loss or say, "You already asked/told me that." Kindly say the answer again, or better yet, in a different way. Ideas to reply are, "That's interesting," or "I'm glad to know that," etc. Pretend like it's the first time you've heard it, reply with "You don't say" or "How about that?", even smile and say "Wow, how interesting" if you're hearing an absurd comment. You may also say, "You might be right," or even, "Tell me more," which will often distract them because they usually can't tell you more; they've forgotten how. Instead of frustration, use creative replies to calmly redirect or distract them, as frustration is not the correct response to someone who is sick, though it is certainly understandable to be irritated. The DP is already frustrated with themselves; be careful not to add to it. Sometimes, a simple touch or a hug is enough to comfort them and can even stop the repetition. Yet, if the cycle persists, for your serenity, you can put your earbuds in or headphones on and happily listen to something else while smiling and nodding at the DP.

Investigate one word that they're saying over again; it could be the key for you. Their vocabulary is significantly reduced. If they keep saying, "You're mean", it may be that they are saying that dementia is mean; it may not be about you. If it's, "Not going to", that could mean they don't know how to, so you'll need to show them one step at a time. If it's "Pokes, sticky," it could be that they need their hands washed. "It nose, it nose" could be something that smells bad.

Learning to allow real or imagined offenses, roll off your back, not even take the bait offered, or be excessively irritated is necessary. Taking an offense is optional, especially when it is not intentional. If you can be unoffendable there will be less need to arm yourself with emotional protection. Yet we are all human, and it is difficult to be bulletproof, so to speak. If you can recognize the triggers to losing one's temper and thus prevent painful regrets, it can become a habit to readily pardon the *offender* and be quick to forgive them and yourself if necessary, and move on. I will say this more than once, and it is so important to repeat to yourself: It is **dementia talking/doing,** so it is, once again, inappropriate to get upset at their symptoms. Most offenses come from damaged expectations; offense is the surprise brought on by the expectation that people will not hurt you. Pastor Charles Swindoll suggested that *Life is 10% what you make it and 90% how you take it.*

They may also become less cantankerous or offensive, so enjoy this if it is your experience. I've heard it said that a caregiver's mother with dementia was like a "declawed cat", meaning she was no longer so mean and no longer fiercely lashed out just to be hurtful.

Since your DP is becoming a very different person from what they used to be, some former expectations must be shelved. Your DP may not understand completely what you're saying about topics they once knew and were interested in. Their ability to converse about a subject has started to dissipate. This can be a harsh reality for you to acknowledge, but you'll need to adapt. They may find interest in different, simpler things now or say little to nothing as time goes on. You may try steering them toward another topic or let the silence stand.

For those times when you are emotionally triggered, one can do a few things:

> This will calm the central nervous system. First, walk away and practice taking deep 4*4*4* breaths. Close your eyes if possible and take a deep breath through your nose while you count slowly to four. Hold it for four counts, then exhale through your mouth for four counts. Finally, stay without breathing for four counts, and then repeat these steps. This is basic physiology and works quite well.

Try these options too, or do what works best for you: If the DP is safe, take a break to another room, go outside to enjoy nature's beauty, call a wise friend to vent, read something positive and meditate on it, turn on classical or soothing music, scream into a pillow &/or punch a pillow, go for a peaceful brisk walk, go ride a bike if you can, or have someone rub your shoulders. Be kind to yourself, and do not be a victim of negative self-talk. Remember, **you** are listening. (Emmet Fox) Refuse to allow *stinking thinking* to interfere with your emotional sobriety. What we say to ourselves is more powerful than what others may say about us. Detach emotionally by doing what calms you or watch a funny TV show or a comic on YouTube, and always pray earnestly.

"A merry heart does good like medicine." - Proverbs 17:22 says,

"Everyone should be quick to listen, slow to speak, and slow to become angry because human anger does not produce the righteousness that God desires." - James 1:19-20.

"God loves you and has chosen you as his own special people. So be gentle, kind, humble, meek, and patient. Put up with each other, and forgive anyone who does you wrong, just as Christ has forgiven you. Love is more important than anything else. It is what ties everything completely together." - Colossians 3:12-14.

3

BUILDING YOUR SUPPORT NETWORK: UTILIZING LOCAL, FAITH AND ONLINE COMMUNITIES

The caregiver's innovative role embodies not just the provision of care but the preservation of dignity as you face dementia's challenges. This feat cannot be done alone, it requires teamwork. An *I can do this alone* attitude is magnified by the relentless demands and unique changes that dementia brings. The antidote, potent yet often overlooked, lies in the pursuit of connection with fellow caregivers. This connection of shared experience serves as a securing anchor, stabilizing each one against the rough winds of change. Your caregiving community offers not just camaraderie but a mirror reflecting the universal nature of your struggles and victories. These communities can remind you to protect your God-given boundaries. Dr. Henry Cloud reminds us that self-awareness is crucial for setting healthy boundaries for ourselves to avoid burnout. "By tuning into the signals our minds and bodies give us, we can navigate life's challenges more effectively. Prioritizing rest, relationships, and activities that recharge us is key to building resilience." (Boundaries.me, Cloud)

This is the season to reach out and ask for some help, even for an hour a day. Some of your dearest friends are clueless about how to help but want to. You'll need to ask them to be there for you and be clear about what they can do. **Never assume**, be direct about what this looks like. It is common to think that the best sources are friends you know already, but this is not always the case. There are new wise friends you haven't met yet; God may be preserving these precious people for this season in your life. Yet, some of your current friends may indeed be there for you whether you ask them to or not. Their presence is powerful enough in many situations, as actions or words are not always necessary. This poem by Gillian Jones describes a dear friend. I hope you have or will cultivate a garden of them.

A friend is like a flower, a rose to be exact, or maybe like a brand new gate that never comes unlatched.
A friend is like an owl, both beautiful and wise. Or perhaps a friend is like a ghost, whose spirit never dies.
A friend is like those blades of grass you can never seem to mow, standing straight, tall, and proud in a perfect little row.
A friend is like a heart that goes strong until the end. Where would we be in this world if we didn't have a friend?

Though often you will need help, one way they can do so is by doing some house cleaning or laundry. If even one or two items are off your list of chores, you can better handle the multiple tasks of caring for your person with dementia. This way they can help you without necessarily giving personal care to your DP, though it is such important care. If you have always been the one to give and serve, now it's your turn to receive. There may come a time when you will return the favors.

If you are not near people geographically, it is especially important to reach out to an acquaintance or neighbor for much-needed human contact. Isolation is not healthy for you or your DP. It can diminish what strength you have. It is one of the deadliest schemes of our adversary to get us alone and begin to think that no one cares, even God. It is a blatant lie. Everyone goes through a wilderness season; even Christ Himself was in the wilderness for 40 days as a model for us, see Matthew 4:1-11. He was triumphant, of course, as He used His Word itself to overcome Satan's temptation. If God Himself wants other people, so do we!

"For as the body is one and has many members, but all the members of that one body, being many, are one body, so also *is* Christ. But now indeed *there are* many members, yet one body. And the eye cannot say to the hand, "I have no need of you," nor again the head to the feet, "I have no need of you." No, much rather, those members of the body which seem to be weaker are necessary. And those *members* of the body which we think to be less honorable, on these we bestow greater honor..."

"But God composed the body, having given greater honor to that part which lacks it, that there should be no schism in the body, but that the members should have the same care for one another. And if one member suffers, all the members suffer with it, or if one member is honored, all the members rejoice with it." - I Corinthians 12:12 & 20-26

3.2. Inviting missed friends or family to visit. Unfortunately, dementia's shadow looms large in conversations, which, once deemed ordinary, now assume a mantle of discomfort, particularly those centered around the reluctance of friends and family to visit. Articulating and initiating these discussions requires both a depth of understanding and a breadth of courage on both sides.

Again, they may not know it is suitable for them to visit the DP, and that they are very welcome. Still, the gradual retreat of familiar faces unfolds with a quiet sorrow. These friends are deterred by the truth of dementia's relentless advance and their fear of how to communicate or if they'll even be recognized anymore. In addition to asking a friend to help clean part of the house or do laundry, here is another simple but very helpful suggestion: ask a friend (different friends on different occasions) to stop at the store to pick up a few items you may need. When they arrive, pay them back and have them bring the grocery bag in and put it in the kitchen. Have your DP come in and say hello. This way, the DP gets (familiar) human contact, and the friend feels less awkward around the DP. It has multiple positive results: you get the groceries you need, the DP gets a moment of friendliness, and you get a potential short-term respite caregiver in the future. This works with any similar request: asking for a church bulletin, requesting them to pick up a prepaid order at Home Depot, or going to retrieve the pet at the vet, etc. Personalize all these requests. A good friend will not turn you down. They want to help, and you've shown them how to. Ask them to sit for a few minutes before they must leave. They may share precious moments with you both and tell you that they can do this favor any time. As Cesare Pavese said, "We do not remember days, we remember moments."

Some clear and direct answers tell them that the warmth of human connection remains a beacon of hope and is very much desired. It is best not to wait till your DP is in a facility to ask friends to visit. The transition to a professional care facility would not be as uncomfortable or awkward if they were regular home visitors. To borrow a quote used by Glen Campbell concerning visitors when he was in his middle stage of Alzheimer's, *"The people that mind don't matter, and the people that matter don't mind."* (Campbell, 2020, p. 210)

3.3. The best advice is to join a communion of caregivers. A silent symphony finds its melody in an orchestra of caregivers that spans the breadth of experience and emotion inherent in this role. Within this community, the act of connecting with peers transcends mere social interaction, it is a lifeline that sustains, empowers, and enlightens. Caregivers truly are missionaries on the front line of a battle with dementia. The hard truth is that in isolation, dementia caregivers run the risk of developing true clinical depression or other life-depleting physical or psychological illnesses. When the caregiver is alone too much with a constant barrage of tasks, a side effect is we may invite "woodpeckers" into our mind. Woodpeckers are noisy hole-punching troublemakers. Woodpeckers are a symbol of damaging self-sabotage, or negative, complaining self-talk, if we listen to and ruminate on them. The best action is to shove them out and replace the damaging thoughts with beneficial thoughts. One of the best places to find this is in the caregiving community. Try to picture positive self-talk as a dove of peace. Feed the dove, deny the other.

There is relief, hope, and comfort in the community. Together, we offer solutions in the shared journey through the trials and triumphs of caregiving. It must be a goal to find a specific small group or community of other dementia caregivers to meet in person, if possible. Join different online ones too, both local and distant. The local ones will have resource information that applies to your situation and location. The distant groups may have excellent support and data for you and your DP, so do not disregard them.

In most faith communities, dementia and its most well-known form, Alzheimer's disease, is, unfortunately, not a part of the established care or prayer team in a religious organization such as a church or synagogue. This is an enormous, missed opportunity that is often due to not being aware of the need. This can change in your community if someone identifies and shares the need for loving, practical support. You've already got enough on your plate to do, that is for certain, but if you can delegate one or two contact people you know, they can address this concern at your place of worship or other houses of worship near you, especially the larger ones. This may be a role for the adult family member to spearhead if they cannot regularly help you in person. Assure this person how important this task is and do not give up or cave to obstacles.

If they reach a contact and can't get help, they may ask who else to speak to and where. It may take several phone calls to the Care Pastor, Assistant Pastor, Priest, Deacon, etc., to set up this important support system and promote it too. Some churches have parish nurses who can coordinate resources within the church congregation.

It may be more appealing to suggest the idea of this group is to be reciprocal. To be and share caregiving responsibilities with others with different kinds of disabilities. This may not sound like a respite for you, but it is a change and may work out okay for a while. Though time by yourself is also needed. Additionally, you may meet people who know other dementia caregivers with whom you can network. Also, be willing to consider a group that already exists for a different purpose, such as generic groups for disability caregivers, widows/widowers, retired people, young professionals, men's or women's groups, or any Bible study. If it is a spiritually healthy group, they will be happy to welcome and support you or at least listen to you and offer ideas.

"...speaking the truth in love, may grow up in all things into Him who is the head—Christ— from whom the whole body, joined and knit together

by what every joint supplies, according to the effective working by which every part does its share, causes growth of the body for the edifying of itself in love." - Ephesians 4:15-16

"Therefore, whatever you want men to do to you, do also to them, for this is the Law and the Prophets." - Matthew 7:12

3.4. Here are tips on finding the right support group that matches your needs, whether it's online or in your community. To seek help when it gets overwhelming is a show of wisdom and strength. It is not caving to pressures; it is filling your tank for the next leg of the journey. The search for a support group that resonates on a personal level is a quest for clarity and connection amid the cacophony of options. The key lies in identifying groups that align not just with logistical considerations such as location and timing but with the emotional and experiential nuances of each caregiver's journey. This group may change over time due to your unique set of circumstances.

Also, ask your primary care physician or your insurance company to give you a good recommendation to a social worker or a case manager through the DP's insurance company. A social worker is not just for people *down on their luck.* They know about public and private resources to help with the DP and support services for you. Talking to a Gerontological or Medical and Health Social Worker may produce some otherwise unknown benefits. Community centers, hospitals, some churches, and online platforms offer a multitude of for-profit and non-profit groups, each with its focus — be it the stage of dementia, the relationship to the person being cared for, or specific challenges faced. The process can unveil niches of solidarity and understanding, two things you will certainly need.

In a group setting, it is always wise to remember to take what you want and leave the rest. Not every person will make a valuable contribution. Be selective with whom you share your pain and frustrations or needs; not all listeners have altruistic motives. Some may interject nonsense or silly opinions that add stress or blame to you, not relieve it. Misery really does love company, so be aware of and alert to who you listen to for encouragement. You, too, will be able to talk compassionate truths to others and find they will value your experiences, stories, and warnings. Some need this setting to vent, and on occasion, that may be you as well. It is perfectly ok, but not habitually. This group should mostly be solutions-oriented rather than problem-focused.

The vastness of the internet has become a fertile ground for caregivers seeking knowledge, solace, and camaraderie. Within these digital realms, caregivers find a way out of isolation through a collective voice that speaks with the authority of lived experience. These resources range from articles penned by dementia specialists offering cutting-edge insights into care strategies. Reading other's personal blogs that chronicle day-to-day victories and setbacks with raw honesty often helps. Forums hum with activity, questions posted find answers, and stories shared ignite discussions that bridge distances and thwart loneliness. This digital companionship offers a balm to the soul, reminding caregivers that you are not alone. A few people on the site may not be entirely pure, so be alert for wolves in sheep's clothing. However, this is common anywhere on the internet. Vigilantly guard your personal information no matter who you talk to or how nice they seem.

Meeting and sharing your story with good people of similar circumstances is therapeutic and makes you a better caregiver. Other emotionally healthy groups have amazing results for all people, regardless of any substance abuse, like Alanon & Celebrate Recovery. These kinds of fellowships work for caregivers, too. You will find solace and knowledge in the shared experiences and mutual understanding that permeates these spaces. Here, a collective strength flourishes amidst peers who navigate the complexities of caring for others while tending to their own wounds. There is a cathartic release in sharing your stories and hearing others share theirs as well. Participation in these groups underscores the recognition that healing and support are not solitary endeavors but communal, guiding the caregiver towards emotional wellness and, thus, lasting capacity for care.

There are several social media support groups; I recommend joining a Dementia and/or Alzheimer's Caregiver Facebook group or Betterhelp.com for relatable comradery, resources, and therapeutic support. Hundreds of thousands all over the world have already joined. Find the one(s) right for you. Keep the online forum as supplemental; generally speaking, it may not be as beneficial as an in-person group. But if that is what you have where you are, make them your new family of choice.

"Be devoted to one another in love. Honor one another above yourselves. Never be lacking in zeal, but keep your spiritual fervor, serving the Lord. Be joyful in hope, patient in affliction, faithful in prayer. Share with the Lord's people who are in need. Practice hospitality. Bless those who persecute you; bless and do not curse. Rejoice with those who rejoice; mourn with those who mourn. Live in harmony with one another. Do not be proud but be willing to associate with people of low position." - Romans 12:10-16

3.5. Regularly participating in support groups can provide emotional relief and practical caregiving strategies. In the ebbs and tides of caregiving, you may get stuck in valleys of monotony and mountains of responsibility, where the burden seems too heavy to bear alone. Being a dementia caregiver involves great personal sacrifice for the sake of your loved one, but the goal is not to sacrifice yourself to the point where your own life is gone. "A full 30% of caregivers die before their dementia patient does."

(AgingCare.com) Over time, unrelieved stress has detrimental effects on the body, the mind, and emotions. If you are unwell or die, what happens to your DP? Seeking others is one answer for your longevity.

These sanctuaries of solace become a lifeline offering practical support and spiritual nourishment, reinforcing your resilience. A few are now or will become like family to you. The collective strength found in fellowship, in sharing burdens, and in uplifting prayer fortifies the spirit, enabling you to persist with your calling as a dementia caregiver. The act of showing up, of being present with those who traverse the same rugged terrain, somehow cuts the weight of the tasks in half. Over time, the benefits compound, transforming the support group from a mere meeting into a safe place for emotional relief and practical caregiving strategies, where burdens are lightened because they are shared.

"And let us consider one another in order to stir up love and good works, not forsaking the assembling of ourselves together, as is the manner of some, but exhorting one another and so much more as you see the day approaching." - Hebrews 10:24-25

3.6. Sharing one's narrative within the safe confines of a support group unfolds as a catharsis and a release of the pent-up emotions and unspoken realities of the caregiving journey. While vulnerable, this sharing is a key that unlocks the bolts of isolation, inviting others into one's world with a level of honesty that promotes deep connections and mutual healing. The stories varied in their details, but universal themes of love, loss, frustration, anxiety, grief, humor, resilience, hope, etc., serve as both a mirror and a window — that offer glimpses into the diverse ways dementia impacts lives. You will find solace and empowerment, the realization that your voice matters, your story resonates, and your journey contributes to the wisdom and success of the group.

I shared with my group about my situation with my DP and her difficulty after being released from the hospital. She had lost her footing and fell which added some additional mobility battles. My group came around to help me in tangible ways while she was on the mend. It was amazing to see their love in action, and it enabled me to go about my routine instead of spending much of my time helping her transfer, bathe, and with toileting issues. I believe having the extra hands helped her heal faster and helped me become a better caregiver. Yet not every day was filled with a volunteer. If there are not enough people who can help out for free, then another source is to seek out someone for a few days or weeks that you hire. Ask friends on **Facebook** and neighbors on the **Nextdoor.com app**, or go to **Care.com** and find a temporary caregiver's assistant on the unfilled calendar days or hours. If you don't know the person, always get references and ask if they are bonded or certified.

"I, therefore, the prisoner for the Lord, urge you to live worthily of the calling with which you have been called, with all humility and gentleness, with patience, putting up with one another in love, making every effort to keep the unity of the Spirit in the bond of peace." - Ephesians 4:1-3

3.7. A support group has all kinds of practical ideas for you and the DP. One of these is to ask what you can do with your DP while you are at your in-person support meeting or spending an hour in your online group. They have a DP too, so they will have valid solutions. Each situation has its own uniqueness to consider. Sometimes caregivers take turns being with the DP, or a friend comes to your home to stay for an hour or two. There will be creative answers if you ask. Some groups bring their DP, and they enjoy the supervised time with other people with varying levels of dementia but are not mixed in with the caregivers. If your group is online, join a group that meets when your DP has an appointment or takes a nap, etc. Your group will have additional answers for you.

In these meetings, you can ask for opinions on how they go grocery shopping or if they use Instacart or home delivery. One answer is, depending on the severity of the stage the DP is at, they can go with you and walk beside you. It may even be a beneficial outing for your DP. Or if your grocery store has a power chair with a cart attached, this is where the DP sits and rides along right next to me. This is only done in the early stage, as it is the DP who has control of the chair's navigation, which is obvious to imagine potential problems. However, I do validate that shopping alone is best due to all kinds of distractions and issues, like forgetting some food or other items while focusing on your DP. When you're alone, getting what you need on your list is much faster and easier. This shopping trip may be one of those reciprocal days with a friend. "You watch my gal/guy while I shop, and I'll do the same for you." More in the next Chapter.

"Let nothing be done through selfish ambition or conceit, but in lowliness of mind let each esteem others better than himself. Let each of you look out not only for his own interests but also for the interests of others." - Philippians 2:3-4

4

THE POWER OF RESPITE CARE: TAKING TIME FOR YOURSELF

R espite care is a necessity lest you drown in the ceaseless tide of responsibilities. The initial steps to securing interval care are strewn with logistical factors, yet it opens up with clarity once the decision to seek aid is made. This is where family can be so important to engage on the front lines of care, if even for a brief period of time. Usually, the DP is much more comfortable with family than an outside caregiver. But if a member of your family or a trustworthy friend is unavailable or unable to help for a few hours a week, there are other sources to go to. Initiating this process involves tapping into a network of resources, from religious to local community services to specialized online listings to national organizations dedicated to supporting individuals with dementia and their caregivers. A skilled social worker can help steer you in the right direction. Private insurance or Medicare coverage and plans vary widely. Your local Medicare agent can help find out what your insurance plan will cover. This may vary state by state. Maybe a family member who cannot help physically can do the research and speak to the agent. Other family members could supplement the funds needed for this vital respite time if not covered by insurance, especially if you are the primary caregiver.

Three of these options are:

1) Part-time (once or twice a week) in-home trained professionals who can step into your shoes after working alongside your DP and you for training. This is someone who comes to your home at a regular interval to take over for you so you can get some time away.

Seek these places to find part-time, interval, or live-in help: **Care.com,** and ask your neighbors on **Nextdoor.com.** Go to **National Respite Network and Resource Center (ARCH)** archrespite.org , **AARP**; www.aarp.org, **Sittercity** @ sittercity.com or **Comfort Keepers** @ comfortkeepers.com. Always vet the person who comes into your home as much as possible.

2) There are short-term stays in residential care facilities, often called Adult Day Care (ADC), where individuals with dementia can be tended to in a fully equipped environment all day, overnight, or for several nights. Be sure to check these out before leaving your DP there. Take or transfer your DP to a recommended, trusted ADC facility for half a day at first, though start with a trial period. Some ADCs offer free or low-cost shuttle service. If you find a church related ADC ministry that is professionally staffed and equipped, this is a rare opportunity to be considered.

Many dementia-supportive places are an excellent source for you to schedule regularly. Your DP will enjoy structured activities, recreation, mealtimes, or afternoon tea and listen to music or a variety of entertainment in a communal setting. Hopefully they will establish new friends and not excessively resist your efforts to get them there. This takes some preplanning visits to see for yourself, alone at first, then with the DP, to watch how things are run, see what's available, and to determine if it's a good fit.

3) Have a good friend or family member you already trust take your place for several hours, with or without pay. Depending on the relationship, I recommend some remuneration for them, so you can maintain an atmosphere like a job commitment, and they will remain reliable and without regrets or resentment. This friend or family member may or may not be live-in. A professional or independent in-home assistant means they live with you but have their own room and a salary. This person will take time to train and get acclimated before you can leave the DP alone with them. Often, they are not married, and your home becomes their place of residence. This means they are on-call all the time except for their day(s) off. On their off day, they leave in the morning and return in the evening, or however you work it out. The workdays, salary, utilities, and food costs are negotiable. It benefits you as a trustworthy full-time caregiver is available to delegate tasks to around-the-clock, 5-6 days a week. This arrangement benefits the assistant as they will have no rent and can save money. This in-home care option becomes essential when the DP is in a moderate to late stage or when you are exhausted and close to depletion without enough help. Obviously, a separate bedroom is required for this to work. However, if needed, there are creative ways to make an office, dining room, den, basement, etc. into a private bedroom. An armoire, large dresser, or shelving should suffice if there is no built-in closet. These can be bought unassembled at stores like Ikea or gently used at Facebook Marketplace, at a garage sale, etc. This would be the responsibility of the assistant to go get.

4) You can also ask private care assistant companies for leads at **A Place for Mom, Visiting Angels, Elder Care, Home Instead,** and, as always, the **Alzheimer's Association**. These sites provide specialized, somewhat vetted caregivers equipped to handle the

complexities of dementia care. They might do respite care, though it depends entirely upon their job circumstances, their availability, and your needs. Talk to a few and find out, and if they can't help you, ask for other colleagues to call who may do respite care.

I suggest you request references from whomever you make an appointment with and call them. If you use a business, such as an ADC, they most likely have a Google Review page. Check these reviews to confirm that the majority of reviews report that it is a safe and beneficial place for your DP.

"Therefore, we do not lose heart. Though outwardly we are wasting away, yet inwardly we are being renewed day by day." - II Cor. 4:16

4.2. Other respite care options. A common option in the early stages is to make arrangements with members of your support group that you cycle through 2 days a week in a kind of reciprocal barter system. You will need to agree to stay with their DP for the same preset amount of time. If there are more than two people in this little group, then each rotation will have the same time away and only one time with another friend's DP. One benefit of this is that there's no fee involved. It might also be nice for your DP to have some company one day on a regular basis. Your DP may behave differently when there's company, either better or worse. The other DP must be calm and somewhat easy to handle. If they are already friends, it may work out well. But if double is too much for you as a caregiver, it defeats the goal entirely. This reciprocal system only works if each caregiver is trustworthy, reliable, and capable of handling two DPs at a time, not three.

Each of these options serves the dual purpose of ensuring the person with dementia continues to receive attentive care while granting their primary caregiver a precious interval of reprieve. This temporary handover of duties is not an act of relinquishment but a strategic retreat, allowing the caregiver to replenish their strength and sustain their capacity to provide care over the long term. After all, the job of a DP caregiver is full-time and then some. This cannot be sustained over a long period without personal damage. Take or get them to an ADC or find respite caregivers, a paid companion, or a medically needed home health aide, at minimum once a week for a half day; 4-6 hours or more, but twice a week is better.

"And whatever you do, do it heartily as to the Lord, not unto men. Knowing that from the Lord you will receive the reward of the inheritance; for you serve the Lord God." - Colossians 3:23-24.

"Then they came to Him, bringing a paralytic who was carried by four men. And when they could not come near Him because of the crowd, they uncovered the roof where Jesus was. So when they had broken through, they let down the bed on which the paralytic was lying." - Mark 2:3-4

4.3. Some of the signs indicate it's time to take a break and how respite care can help prevent caregiver burnout. Dr. Henry Cloud says, "Pain is our body's way of telling us that something is wrong and needs attention. Yet, we often push through discomfort to get by, not realizing the long-term consequences. Ignoring this internal alarm clock can lead to overextension, depletion, and limited lives." (Boundaries.me) Being in physical pain is the red light on your dashboard announcing that something is wrong; do not ignore it for very long. Even though the crucible of caregiving seldom affords its bearers the luxury of pause, it can often blur the lines between dedication and depletion. Recognizing the signals that herald the need for a break is thus a critical regular practice.

These 19 signs are valid indicators of burnout:

- Pervasive sense of fatigue that sleep does not alleviate, and caffeine no longer helps

- Persistent feelings of sadness or depression
- Prolonged anxiety
- Feelings of emotional detachment or numbness
- Feelings of guilt and resentment
- Difficulty concentrating
- Decreased productivity
- The dawning realization that the days have melded into a monotonous stream
- Becoming irritable and unreasonable without even knowing it
- Loss of interest in hobbies or favorite activities
- Frequent illness
- Loss of appetite or weight
- Being absent-minded or forgetful ourselves
- Neglecting personal needs
- Abuse of substances to self-medicate negative feelings
- Feelings of hopelessness or excessively angry
- Growing emotional outbursts, rage, or quick temper
- Going between moments of apathy and anxiety
- Blaming God or increasing doubts about His love

These distress flares indicate that the caregiver's well-being is in jeopardy. The acknowledgment of any of these symptoms serves as the first step toward seeking respite care, you do not need to have them all to make a change and get help. It is a vital recognition that to continue to pour out care, the caregiver's vessel must first be repaired and refilled. It is highly probable that your DP would not only want you to take a beneficial break but insist on it. Keep this in mind: If you don't take a break, **you** will eventually break. This book is filled with ideas for how to best care for yourself which has the additional benefit of being a better, more effective caregiver.

"The Lord is my shepherd; I shall not want. He makes me to lie down in green pastures; He leads me beside the still waters. He restores my soul; He leads me in the paths of righteousness for His name's sake. Yea, though I walk through the valley of the shadow of death, I will fear no evil; for You are with me; Your rod and Your staff, they comfort me. You prepare a table before me in the presence of my enemies; You anoint my head with oil; my cup runs over. Surely goodness and mercy shall follow me all the days of my life; and I will dwell in the house of the Lord, forever." - Psalm 23.

4.4. How taking regular breaks can improve your caregiving by allowing you to recharge and return to caregiving duties with renewed energy. The infusion of respite into the caregiver's routine casts ripples across the surface of their caregiving experience, its effects are profound and manifold. A respite period, whether spent in quiet solitude, engaging in neglected personal interests, or simply in the pursuit of sleep, acts as a balm to the weary spirit. Maybe a kind neighbor, someone the DP may know, would allow you to take a nap for a couple of hours in their home while they watch the DP in your home. Our modern world makes too many people sound hideous, selfish, and untrustworthy, but kind, generous people do still exist. A simple thank you note will be received with joy. Often, good respite care is just a call away. If you are still hesitant to ask for help, first ask yourself, why? What takes priority over caring for yourself? Good self-care is not selfish, it is the opposite. If you are unable to care for another person, returning to that sense of well-being and capability is paramount. Maybe you will need to swallow your pride and realize that even if this respite caregiver doesn't do it exactly the way you've always done it, their style is not the most important thing. Your whole health is! Besides, they may have a better or different way of doing something you've never thought of. Being flexible brings relief.

In the moments of respite tranquility, you'll be reminded of your identity beyond the current role, rediscovering the joys and passions that nourish your soul. The return to caregiving duties after such an interlude is marked by a renewal of energy and clarity of perspective. The care provided in this rejuvenated state is enriched, the patience is deeper, the understanding is broader, and the connection with their loved one is fortified. In its essence, respite care serves as a demonstration of the understanding that to give care sustainably, one must also receive care, nurturing the caregiver's resilience and ensuring the continuity of compassionate, attentive support for their loved one.

"The everlasting God, the Lord, the Creator of the ends of the earth, neither faints nor is weary. His understanding is unsearchable. He gives power to the weak, and to those who have no might, He increases strength. Even the youths shall faint and be weary, and the young men shall utterly fall, but those who wait on the Lord shall renew their strength; they shall mount up with wings like eagles, they shall run and not be weary, they shall walk and not faint." - Isaiah 40: 28b-31

5

COMMUNICATING YOUR NEEDS
TO FAMILY AND FRIENDS

S trategies for effectively communicating your needs and seeking support from family and friends. In the maze of caregiving, where days meld into nights in a seamless continuum of tasks and responsibilities, articulating one's own needs becomes an act of bravery. Your determination to give the highest quality of care begins with reaching out for help. Many caregivers make the mistake of trying to shelter our families from the cruel realities of the disease. (Fantasia, 2014, p. 85) Communicating these needs to family and friends is of utmost importance. Each person can do their share to unburden you with the intrinsic human need for support and understanding. Periodic family discussions by phone, facetime, or in person can be very helpful in keeping the family up to date on DP's progress or decline. Strategies for this delicate disclosure involve timing conversations to coincide with moments of calm, ensuring the waters of communication are as still as possible. Timing is critical for respecting others' boundaries and for getting positive feedback or results. Do not jump in *like a bull in a china shop.* Make an appointment and follow through.

If things get heated, do not use "You" statements. They are aggressive and blame-led. They often accompany the absolute terms "always" or "never," which are very rarely true. Statements like, "You never"... abort any genuine attempts at understanding or empathy. Instead, use statements that begin with "I". Employing "I" statements serves as a bridge, allowing people their feelings and needs without casting shadows of blame or expectation on their listeners. It is difficult to argue with one's sincere feelings when the caregiver says, "I feel...".

When delivered with clarity and sincerity, this articulation opens the door to understanding, inviting those within one's circle to step into the caregiver's world, if only for a moment, to see the rugged landscape through their eyes.

5.2. Digital tools can help maintain connection and thus fortify the family wherever they are. If your family is far away, has small children, or works a consistent schedule, then a video **Zoom call, Apple's Facetime** or **Google Duo** is a pleasant link for you and your DP. WhatsApp is an good choice for overseas links. Others, such as **Viber, Google Meet, Skype, Microsoft Teams,** or **Facebook Messenger live,** may also work well for you. Some of these must be installed and set up ahead of time. Video calling platforms diminish the miles that separate families, their screens windows into the lives of loved ones, ensuring that faces and voices remain familiar despite the distance.

"Finally, all of you be of one mind, having compassion for one another; love as brothers, be tenderhearted, be courteous; not returning evil for evil or reviling for reviling, but on the contrary blessing, knowing that you were called to this, that you may inherit a blessing." - I Peter 3:8-9.

5.2. Establishing family and friends' boundaries and what are they? According to Dr. Henry Cloud and Dr. John Townsend, "boundaries set the personal property lines that delineate where one person ends, and another begins." (Cloud & Townsend, 1992, p. 25) Healthy, loving boundaries ensure relationships are based on mutual respect and understanding. Boundaries help individuals take responsibility for their own lives and actions, not others. Boundaries provide freedom by protecting individuals from the improper actions of others and by giving them the space to make their own choices. Setting boundaries is for you and your DP, not disciplining family members. Good emotional and physical boundaries help resolve family conflicts.

The importance of setting healthy boundaries to manage the expectations of your DP and your family is not one of division but of preservation. It serves as a tribute to the caregiver's self-awareness and recognition of their limits. These boundaries often look like this pattern: "I will do this for this long, but not this." Or something like, "I will do the laundry but not mow the grass." Or "I will change the lightbulbs but not the Air Conditioner's filter."

This demarcation of boundaries is an essential strategy to manage expectations—both the caregiver's own and those of the family unit. (Cloud & Townsend, 1992) Establishing these limits involves a deep introspection, a journey inward to identify the non-negotiables that sustain the caregiver's well-being and the quality of care they provide. It might mean specifying visiting hours that do not disrupt the care routine or clearly stating tasks one is unable to shoulder alone. This conversation, approached with honesty and anchored in the necessity of maintaining the caregiver's health, fosters a mutual respect for the caregiver's role and a shared commitment to the well-being of the loved one with dementia. Loose or those with no boundaries are often "yes men" or "people pleasers" who deny themselves the right to say "no". This kind usually ends up with ineffective work and with bitter resentments as their motive is not really altruistic.

"But let your 'Yes' be 'Yes,' and your 'No,' 'No.'" - Matthew 5:37.

5.3. Tips on how to ask for help in specific, actionable ways that make it easier for others to provide the support you need. This is geared toward family, but it applies to anyone.

In the realm where caregivers often find themselves isolated on an island of responsibility, reaching out for assistance is a beacon that cuts through the fog of solitude. The key to effective assistance lies not in useless or whiny vague pleas but in crafting specific, actionable requests.

This precision transforms the hazy into the attainable, providing family and friends with a clear pathway to lend their support. When asking for help, remember this pattern: *say what you mean, mean what you say, but don't say it mean.* It could manifest in asking for someone to take over meal preparations on specific days, requesting a companion for doctor's visits, or seeking someone to stay with the loved one as they engage in their favorite activity so you can do another task. This specificity acts as a map, guiding willing hands to tasks where their efforts are most needed, ensuring that the gesture of support is both meaningful and impactful. This verse is specific for widows, but the idea that we are to care for our family members in times of genuine need is clear. Maybe you have no family to help; the church can then step in to be your family.

"If a person who is a believer has relatives who are widows, she must take care of them and not put the responsibility on the church. Then the church can care for the widows who are truly alone, with no relatives." - I Timothy 5:16. NLT

5.4. The family dynamics of dementia care require a blend of diplomacy and honesty, leading with grace while speaking truthfully. It involves recognizing each family member's different capacity for involvement and adjusting expectations to align with reality. This adjustment does not signify a lowering of standards but an acknowledgment of the diverse ways individuals are equipped to contribute according to their proximity, age, health, career, etc. Most adult children of the DP have full time jobs and maybe their own children to care for. For the one person who takes on the primary job as caregiver, they ought to be held in high esteem with much gratitude and no criticism. It is so true that the more you can support the relative caregiver, the more they can do their job well. Ultimately the patient is the benefactor of their caregiver being supported.

If the caregiver is the DP's spouse, the same goes for this as well. However, sometimes the spouse is unable to take on such a monumental job, so if an adult child or a sibling of yours does it, they are truly a blessing. A sibling, niece, nephew, sister-in-law, brother-in-law, etc., of the DP, may also help a lot, especially if they are capable and close in proximity. Family tensions must be shelved for the good of everyone involved in caring for the DP, thereby reducing blame, shame, and isolation.

Being a caregiver can be a thankless job, or at least in the middle and later stages of dementia. Or your DP may start out sweet and grateful, knowing how much you're sacrificing for them. Either way, one's attitude about the enormous task must be seen as a calling from God Himself, not a chore or drudgery to endure. The patient may sense the difference and reflect the negative attitude back. Be like a thermostat rather than a thermometer; set your attitude to a positive one and do not check other's attitudes to join--- unless it's also good. If a family member can help, the DP *may* interpret the part-timer's intentions as negative and become irritable. This obviously makes the job more unpleasant. They also may thoroughly enjoy and value the time spent with this family member if their attitude is wholesome. This scenario is far more prevalent. Time spent with the DP will refine one's own character for the better if we let it. That is one of God's goals here.

"And not only that, but we also glory in tribulations, knowing that tribulation produces perseverance; and perseverance, character; and character, hope. Now hope does not disappoint because the love of God has been poured out in our hearts by the Holy Spirit who was given to us." - Romans 5:3-5.

Engaging in open dialogues about caregiving situations fosters an environment where each voice is heard, and each concern is acknowledged, including sons-in-law, daughters-in-law, and step-children. The aim is to transform potential friction into a unified front. This unity, born from acknowledging individual limitations and celebrating shared goals, is both necessary and appropriate. Realize if or when the family dynamic remains incongruent, then getting help is needed to settle the differences. It may be time to call a family conference with a neutral party to mediate it. It can make the dementia problem much worse if all are not aligned to do the best for the DP, no matter their history. I am certain that the DP would hate it if the family were arguing about them. Be aware of a manipulation technique called triangulation. This occurs when one person communicates with another through a third party, creating a communication triangle, often behind someone's back. Ask that all communications come directly from each person themselves.

"Understand this, my dear brothers and sisters: You must all be quick to listen, slow to speak, and slow to get angry." - James 1:18 NLT

"Bear one another's burdens, and so fulfill the law of Christ." - Galatians 6:2

5.5. Establish a communication plan with family, friends, and emergency responders during an emergency to ensure that in moments of urgency, clarity prevails over confusion. Emergency preparedness is incomplete without preemptive planning. It is essential to know who to call ahead of time if the DP goes missing. Because time is of the essence, it is best to make one call after 911. This person can call other people on your list. They will need a network of contacts, a group of individuals they can rely on in moments of need. This network, expansive in its reach, includes not only family and close friends but also neighbors, health care providers, and local emergency responders, each briefed on the specific requirements and conditions of the person with dementia. The deployment of this plan, facilitated by technology that ensures messages are disseminated swiftly and accurately, becomes a lifeline, bridging the gaps that distance or disorder may impose. In this realm, clarity reigns with protocols for who is contacted first and how information is relayed, ensuring that, amidst the upheaval, a semblance of order is preserved. When making contact with family and friends, first ask for prayer support.

There are other reasons to call 911, such as when the DP falls. Do not try to lift them yourself. Just stay with them on the floor (if you can) and speak calmly, letting them know that strong, skilled people are on their way to help. These people are professionals, and this kind of call is a large part of their job, so there is no reason to be embarrassed. They are all very kind, nonjudgemental, and helpful. Paramedics do more than gently pick the DP up off the floor; they'll ensure he/she has no injuries and take their vital signs.

The specter of emergencies, with their unpredictable fury and potential for chaos, demands a strategy with forethought and calm. Other emergencies require different preparation. If a fire ignites, a tornado alarm goes off, a tsunami or a hurricane warning is issued. The following steps may be the difference between life and death. Your DP may hide in these instances. Be aware and prepared for this. Preparation encompasses the very structure of the environment, where exits are marked clearly and unobstructed by the detritus of daily living. Emergency kits and 72-hour grab-bags for both you and the DP are needed. These are packed with necessities and stand ready at strategic points, their contents filled with the foresight of a calm caregiver. This saves time, energy, and stress to be prepared with these customized grab bags to be kept out of reach but readily available to you or your respite person. Being prepared is not a lack of faith; it is an act of love.

"I sought the Lord, and He heard me and delivered me from all my fears."

"The angel of the Lord encamps all around those who fear Him and delivers them." - Psalm 34: 4&7.

6

PERSONALIZING CARE: ADAPTING TO THEIR CHANGING WORLD

I t is important to create personalized care plans that consider the unique needs and preferences of the individual DP and their caregiver. Both the DP's needs and their caregiver capacities intertwine, demanding a tailored approach to nurturing and support. Here, the caregiver's intuition and knowledge become invaluable, guiding the adaptation of care practices to resonate with the unique rhythms of their loved one's life. Most caregivers are already aware of their DP needs and values and are generally accustomed to putting their loved one's needs above their own. However, this can create caregiver fatigue and ultimate failure, which is not what the caregiver wants nor what the DP would want. Along with scheduled breaks, the caregiver needs their own goals and plans, even if it is only two or three things, for this season of their life. In this endeavor, the scripture, "And the second is like it, you shall love your neighbor as yourself..." Mark 12:31 serves as a poignant reminder of the reciprocal nature of care. Though the caregiver's needs must not be ignored or consistently denied, once you get the rest you need, you can serve the DP so much better and with a contagious positive attitude.

"I can do all things through Christ who strengthens me." - Philippians 4:13

6.2. Incorporating both individuals' hobbies and interests into their daily routine can improve their and your quality of life. This transformation is not merely about loss but about adaptation, finding new pathways to connection and understanding. The caregiver becomes an interpreter, learning to decipher the unspoken and to listen with the heart as well as the ears. This process is as much about valuing the person as it is about practicality, acknowledging the shifting sands of cognitive ability while affirming the inherent value and worth of the individual. Your hobbies and interests that bring joy and fulfillment outside of caregiving duties must be scheduled regularly, as they are as important as the caregiving you give to the DP. Your wants and needs cannot be entirely sacrificed for the DP's sake, as it will most assuredly hurt them in the long run if you are stretched too far without personal self-care maintenance. Physical, emotional, and spiritual caregiver fatigue is real and can be avoided with a team to help take up the slack. A 'they don't do it right, so I will just do it myself' attitude can be a faulty one. Again, prioritize your own well-being as much as your DP's. In the end, remember to ask yourself, "How important is it?" Severe control is not your friend; teach your helpers and then trust them.

This recalibration of care and communication strategies underscores the profound truth that each person, regardless of cognitive decline, possesses an innate dignity and right to be heard and understood. These may be some of the last vestiges of typical life before dementia, and if at all possible, they need to be acknowledged as important to maintain to some degree. Choose wisely of course, if they used to build things with a lathe or power tool, etc., it would be smart to remove these from their accessibility altogether. Or if they love to paint and decorate, the paints will need to be relocated out of reach. If they drove a motorcycle or a sports car, it may be time to sell this vehicle, but take photos of it first to discuss it as a memory of the past. See Chapter 7. Their abilities have shifted, and it has become necessary to shift with it. Your DP is in some ways *like* a child, so ask yourself if you would let a child do the request safely. But, if the hobbies and interests were safe and comforting, do indeed continue these. Notice if they are a source of comfort and normalcy and not frustration or anger.

It is said that *a dog is man's best friend*, this is especially true with someone who has dementia. An animal's unconditional love is extremely evident and beneficial. Most dogs and cats have an uncanny ability to sense their human's pain or when something is wrong, often before the caregiver does. If the DP has a cat, dog, or other pets before the diagnosis, keeping these animals, as long as they are home, is best. If they love dogs or cats, it can be thera-peutic to get one now, though do realize that, especially later on, the pet's care will be mostly up to you or another family member. To eliminate the DP getting lost, you will need to go with them to walk the dog or get someone else to do this regularly. When, or if, the DP goes to live elsewhere, the pet can visit them. This will be a sincere joy and a comfort. Pets have been known to help the DP release those happy dopamine hormones. During the visit, if you see the DP crying when seeing either their animal or a visitor's pet, it is mostly happy tears.

"The righteous care for the needs of their animals," - Proverbs 12:10a.

"And also that every man should eat and drink and enjoy the good of all his labor, it is the gift of God." - Ecclesiastes 3:13

6.3. Adapting care and communication as cognitive abilities change. The DP often remains generally happy and naïve to the situation, but the caregiver sees the decline and differences with eyes wide open. To remind you; caregivers too can begin to decline if good, practical self-care, spiritual care, nutritional, and physical expressions are not regularly sought and practiced. It's the idea of the flight attendant saying to put the oxygen mask on yourself first. The time in the lives of the caregiver and their DP can be a challenge or even a battle as the decline and symptoms progress. These days can seem like a monotonous grind to survive rather than thrive.

Common dementia behaviors are rummaging and repetition, R&R that may interfere with a moment of rest and relaxation; another kind of R&R. Your DP may go through every drawer or cabinet in the home as if searching for something or rearrange things or appear to count simple items over and over for hours. This doesn't harm you but can be a source of irritation. In the scope of dementia, it is a minor nuisance. If your DP does this, it is wise to keep valuable or breakable things locked away or move to another location altogether. Rather than get frustrated with the R&R, use this for good. Try putting new and colorful items to discover (magazines, sweaters, shoes, T-shirts, underwear, pens & pencils, etc.) in their favorite drawers or cabinets. This will often entertain them; it may bring you some delight, too, as you watch them discover shiny new or unexpected things.

With or without monotony, providing and protecting your former way of life is critical as much as possible. Allow for several hours a week for **your** rest and relaxation R&R, doing things that bring normalcy and reduce cabin fever. A respite caregiver is not always necessary for you to do what you used to do. If they are napping, you too should nap or do what you enjoy. Yet, at these times, a shorter break (even to another room) is critical to maintain sanity.

"Are not two sparrows sold for a penny? Yet not one of these falls to the ground outside your Father's care. And even the very hairs of your head

are all numbered. So don't be afraid; you are worth more than many sparrows." - Matthew 10:29-31

6.4. Maintaining your own and the DP's sense of self throughout the caregiving journey is preferred-- when at all possible. In mid or late stages, some DP's often develop an aversion to bathing, either in the shower or tub. They may have a fear of the water, of being cold and/or naked, etc., and cannot speak the terms to tell you. Keep reassuring them that the water is warm but not hot; let them feel it and that you're always with them. Do not fill the tub up very high; accidental slipping is possible, and if it's deep, they could drown in a few moments. As a rule, lower the hot water heater's temperature so it cannot accidentally burn them. Depending upon the relationship, getting in the shower with them might be necessary. Be mindful that they may be shy or modest with entirely undressing. If so, there is a personal care garment that allows one to be washed without exposing them and weakening their dignity. It can be found at Dignity Resource Council's website: https://drc.yolasite.com/honor-guard.php. A bathing suit is an acceptable way to provide needed coverage for the caregiver since it's not you who the shower is for.

Wrangling an adult into the water is unwise due to all kinds of potential slippery accidents. Having them sit in a stationary or a locked-wheeled shower chair is a good option if they stay seated most of the time. While you are both seated, with you on the tub, you may take this time to trim their fingernails and, less often, their toenails. This accomplishes a dual purpose: get the job done and their nails cleaned at the same time. Nevertheless, any of this may be one of those areas where you'll require extra help from someone who is reliable and who is not shy around them nude. If this is needed, schedule this help ahead of time. Most older people with or without dementia require a professional to have their toenails cut to prevent a cut or an infection.

Personal cleanliness requires some creativity and ingenuity, such as providing new, colorful towels or styles of soap to try. If you promote it this way, they may believe the towels are different every time, and that liquid soap is fun. It may be a nice time to add music to bath or shower time. Some people sing in the shower, it's worth a try to get the job done easier.

If none of this works to finish the job, praise and thank them for trying. You can never go wrong with praise. Building them up will help alleviate a bad attitude about the bathing and teeth brushing routine. Then try again later. They may forget the instructions, but not necessarily how you made them feel. This is true for everyone.

6.5 It is important to have the DP's fine motor skills assessed by an Occupational Therapist or OT to see if they can still brush their own teeth with only a little direction. In the earlier and middle stages, they should be able to. I suggest using a traditional non-electric brush, as an electric toothbrush has all kinds of potential fears attached to it. The sounds and actions may make them think it is a painful dental instrument. If they have always used an electric toothbrush, then maybe it will be fine for your DP to continue with it. Just be alert to any hesitations in the future. Pay special attention to teeth that are removable, bridges, partials, etc. Some areas may be very sensitive to cold water or the toothbrush action, which means reluctance to brush any teeth.

Choose joy and humor as ways to be productive. Brushing teeth may also need to be done in unison. If you try to make it a fun experience, it may not be resisted as much. Creativity in hygiene is your friend. Try counting the teeth as each one is "washed." See who can make a foamy mouth first, then have fun taking aim to spit on the sink stopper; you go first. A light, playful attitude is a powerful tool in your toolbox. Yet they may occasionally reject this behavior altogether, so be flexible.

Being creative does not signify capitulation but rather a strategic adaptation, a willingness to meet the individual where they are, affirming them while gently guiding them towards safety, cleanliness, and comfort. In this, caregivers are reminded that the essence of the individual, their inherent worth, remains untouched by the superficial and/or profound changes wrought by dementia. This is steadfast love the scriptures speak of and that you are called into.

6.6 The application of makeup, the selection of clothing, the simple act of styling hair—each becomes an indication to the person who once was and who, in many ways, still is. When at all possible, keep the DP as private and routine in their toileting as one can and still be very safe. There may come a day when they will try to relieve themselves anywhere, any time. This is because they've forgotten universal unspoken rules of going to the bathroom or even what a bathroom is. Urinary incontinence can be an issue with many, so it will be important for you to create awareness of this and periodically ask them if they have a wet pad or incontinence underwear. A strategy of gentleness and creativity is vital in helping them to change it when needed. Not all of these fit tight enough, so some adjustments may be needed. See Chapter 21. Later on, bowel incontinence may also be a problem. This requires you to be especially mindful of not showing excessive disgust when cleaning up. This is accidental and must not be treated with a lot of drama that brings shame or embarrassment to them. It's still another chance to take the high road rather than being mean.

If makeup was worn before dementia, a little bit of make-up can be applied during too, especially if the DP has an outing. Yet, I warn against allowing her to do this task herself if the dementia has interfered with her ability to do it properly. There is no reason to let her look ridiculous. It will become your job if the act of applying a little makeup has been a familiar and soothing routine. As with most people, one's appearance can alter their mood; either good and confident or silly and embarrassed, etc. If she is irritated at your efforts and doesn't seem to care anymore, then toss it aside altogether, or for another day. One more thing about this: makeup, especially red lipstick and dark mascara, can make a hard-to-remove mess in fabrics. Discernment and caution go a long way here. The DP's new routine may need to include only face cream and clear or slightly tinted Burts Bees-type lip gloss.

Their hair needs attention too, especially cleanliness and combing. It does not need to always be a professional styling job, as that may be a low-priority expense. When needed, seek someone who can come to your place and offer a haircut, as a trip out for this may become unmanageable. Shaving, too, may be a daily task that he or she once did but now cannot do safely alone or thoroughly. If shaving was done, keep it up as much as time and safety permits. Otherwise, drop the daily routine to once or twice a week or entirely.

I remember seeing a photo on social media of a small group at a restaurant with an older acquaintance who had middle-stage Alzheimer's; sadly, she looked so very different, hardly recognizable. Her hair was in disarray, her clothes were a wrinkled, unmatched mess, and she had no makeup on. She looked wild and wide-eyed lost. She had always been so put together in every detail, so lovely. I thought to myself, someone could have made just a bit of effort to preserve even a tiny bit of her former appearance and dignity. However, in the eternal realm, these superficial choices are often of low priority. I know that the caregiver's role is to look out for the best interest of the DP. I am sure she would have wanted her appearance to be more like it used to be. She was and is a beautiful godly woman who fears the Lord. Beauty and self-care are not a sin, they are gifts from God. It reminds me of the biblical story of Esther. Hadassah (Esther) was the most beautiful woman in the kingdom, she pleased the king because of this.

God used her appearance, attitude, and courage to save her people from certain death. Yet someone's looks are not the primary concern, it is only subsequent in priority rank.

"Let your adorning be the hidden person of the heart with the imperishable beauty of a gentle and quiet spirit, which in God's sight is very precious" - 1 Peter 3:4.

"Charm is deceptive, and beauty is fleeting; but a woman who fears the LORD is to be praised." - Proverbs 31:30

6.7. Not every DP wants to maintain their former sense of style or routines, it is possible that their previous style may have very well gone out the window entirely. They may be reluctant to put on easy loafer-style shoes, or stretchy pants, etc. They may develop a new, strange style that you dislike. It is not worth a scuffle to deny it, so for the sake of their new ideas and the caregiver's peace, it's better to allow them to wear whatever they may want, as long as it's not grievously inappropriate, such as a tank-top to the mall in the colder months. Compromise is a good thing to practice; they can wear their tank-top under pants or shorts and a jacket. Many layers of buried instincts rise to the surface with DP's. Former filters, norms, and customs have begun to atrophy. This may also occur in many uncomfortable ways, especially in the latter stages. Your DP has or may become less inhibited, as they are freer to experiment with new ideas and want to discard the old. Or this new style may be fleeting and gone the next day. A hefty dose of sensitivity is needed here. Redirection is required if the uninhibited behavior, such as stripping down to their birthday suit and even going outside naked, will inevitably cause the DP or their family embarrassment. This is due to their brain's filter being damaged. It is not right to assume this is a sexual act; it is far more likely that they are uncomfortable, hot, itchy, etc., and took care of the problem in the best way they could. A kind offer for new clothes to put on may get them dressed again. Exposing themselves anywhere requires true tact to eliminate. Words such as, "Put your arm in this soft sweater; it's getting cold." Then, lead them in covering up. If the timing is good, take this opportunity to walk them to a warm shower instead of covering up. Certainly, shaming or scolding them for this newly surfaced behavior, style, or desire is also inappropriate. If it's just style, this can often be an area of disagreement, so some caregiver self-awareness is needed. An attitude check of *how important is it?* goes a long way.

6.8 Humor often helps lessen stressful scenarios. Seek ways to lighten the mood with a smile and distractions to something happy or funny. I suggest an electric Wi-Fi photo frame that the family can periodically upload and share new photos remotely from wherever they are. It is delightful to see the pictures appear in the frame and the screen changes at set intervals. This is a simple yet effective way to distract the DP or happily view anytime. The pictures are usually new to him/her anyway. They can be photos of their children, grandchildren, animals, recent events, holidays, scenes of familiar places, etc. These smart photo frames are found at most stores or online. Look for **Nixplay, Aura, Pix-star, Frameo,** and **Skylight,** etc., to name a few.

Another way to distract them from a stressful time is to point out the window and describe two birds "choosing from their colorful feathered wardrobe" to prepare for the day. Use squirrels, rabbits, lizards, etc., next time. If you're laughing at this imaginary scene, your DP probably will, too.

Most DPs live contentedly in the present, entirely unaware and unencumbered by norms, cultural rules, or even the weather. (Fantasia, 2019) We must check our own feelings of embarrassment if the DP stubbornly refuses to dress as we guide them to. They certainly must miss their autonomy and may try to wrestle it back from us. We must let them on occasion if appearance is the only issue, not safety or weather. Remember, *how important is it?* Many layers of deeper instincts rise to the surface with DP's, not just clothing or other superficial choices. Since the filters have atrophied, unidentified or very old thoughts may surface unabated, such as childhood and youthful memories. This is usually a pleasant, even humorous thing, but could possibly be embarrassing if others are watching. In this verse, God prioritizes the inside character far above the outside when referring to David.

"But the Lord said to Samuel, "Do not look at his appearance or at his physical stature, because I have refused him. For the Lord does not see as man sees; for man looks at the outward appearance, but the Lord looks at the heart." - I Samuel 16:7

7

ADDRESSING DRIVING AND DEMENTIA: MAKING HARD DECISIONS FOR SAFETY

This chapter is a guide on assessing the driving ability of an individual with dementia, including signs when it is time to stop altogether. Several U.S. States require physicians to notify the DMV when a patient is diagnosed with Alzheimer's or has cognitive impairment. Their driver's license will automatically be revoked in those states. Most states rely on voluntary reporting. Signals indicating a reassessment of driving privileges include instances of getting lost in familiar locales, worsening vision or distance calculations, difficulty making quick decisions, ability to move the car over when a siren sounds, poor judgment, confusion at traffic lights, very slow driving, unexplained dents or scratches on the vehicle, and increased agitation or confusion while driving. Such indicators, subtle yet significant, underscore the need for a careful, empathetic approach to evaluating driving ability, ensuring that the safety of the individual and the broader community is preserved. If they are determined to keep this privilege, they can take a driving test at the DMV or get their doctor's permission to drive with a promise to obey these. Then, you are off the hook for the decision. It is far better to eliminate their driving early rather than late.

"Trust in the Lord with all your heart and lean not on your own understanding; In all your ways acknowledge Him, and He shall direct your paths. - Proverbs 3:5-6.

"The Lord will keep you from all evil; he will keep your life. The Lord will keep your going out and your coming in from this time forth and forevermore." - Psalm 121:8

7.2. Tips for having a compassionate yet firm conversation with your loved one about ceasing to drive. Broaching the subject of relinquishing driving privileges with your DP is a conversation laden with emotional weight, often perceived as a direct challenge to their autonomy and independence. The conversation benefits from a private setting, free from distractions, where the individual feels secure and respected. Framing the discussion around concerns for their safety and the safety of others, rather than casting aspersions on their abilities, can ease the reception of this difficult message. Acknowledging the loss that this change may evoke and validate their feelings while gently guiding them toward accepting this new phase in their life is helpful. It is important to explain this change as a choice for a better, longer life with less anxiety. Let them know they will now be chauffeured wherever they want to go. Make them feel honored to be driven around; many DPs love little car trips and now they can look out the windows more.

Once you've made the decision to end their driving privilege, there are many ways to use this asset if there are two or more vehicles. Cars, trucks, motorcycles, or boats can be sold to add practical value to the current bottom line. The extra vehicle may now also be used for a respite caregiver. Maybe ask the DP what they would like to do with the proceeds of the vehicle's sale. Or discuss how much joy it would bring to give their car to a distressed single mom, or a grandchild, etc.

"Do not lay up for yourselves treasures on earth, where moth and rust destroy and where thieves break in and steal; but lay up for yourselves treasures in heaven, where neither moth nor rust destroys and where thieves do not break in and steal. For where your treasure is, there your heart will be also." - Matthew 6: 19-21

7.3. The legal and safety considerations involved in making decisions about driving and dementia, including potential liability issues. The intersection of driving and dementia has legal implications and safety concerns, necessitating a vigilant approach to decision-making in this arena. It is always better to be safe than sorry when it comes to getting behind the wheel of a 4000+ pound moving vehicle. Legal considerations pivot around the individual's competency to drive, a determination that, while influenced by medical assessments and cognitive tests, ultimately falls under the purview of state regulations. Familiarizing oneself with these laws and the process for reporting concerns about a driver's competence is crucial. Moreover, the liability issues at stake for both the individual with dementia and their family members underscore the importance of timely, decisive action in restricting driving when necessary. If the doctor orders the DP to cease driving and you're aware of this, the penalty for an accident they may cause includes you.

As this discussion draws to a close, it beckons us forward, reminding us of the broader picture of dementia care—a landscape where every decision, every conversation, and every transition is infused with love, respect, and the unwavering belief in the value of each individual's journey through dementia's complexities.

"Let the words of my mouth and the meditation of my heart be acceptable in Your sight, O LORD, my strength and my Redeemer." - Psalm 19:14

7.4. Exploring occasional alternative transportation options and how to encourage their use to maintain some kind of independence. The following options may be possible for the DP to do alone, yet it is always much safer and highly recommended that they do **not** go alone on any public transportation even in an early stage. When a trip is scheduled, make sure to schedule a ride-along companion as well.

The cessation of driving does not equate to the end of their independence or mobility entirely. Public transportation, while not suitable for all, may be an option for those in the **earlier** stages of dementia, provided routes and schedules are simple and familiar. Ride-sharing services such as Uber or Lyft, community shuttles designed for seniors, paratransit services, and passenger speed trains offer more personalized solutions while catering to the specific needs of individuals with cognitive impairments. Wise and individual boundaries must be in place to regulate any outgoing activities, even just a ride down the street. Involving the individual in the selection and planning of these alternatives fosters a sense of participation and control, easing the transition from driver to passenger. This shift in mobility options also presents an opportunity to reinforce social connections as family members and friends become more intricately involved in the daily life of the person with dementia.

"The fear of the Lord is pure, enduring forever; the judgments of the Lord are true and righteous altogether." - Psalm 19:9

8

MANAGING MOOD SWINGS AND BEHAVIORAL SHIFTS

With dementia, the brain's pathways undergo a relentless, unpredictable metamorphosis, precipitating fluctuations in mood and behavior that confound and distress both the afflicted and their caregivers. Thus, depression is a common byproduct of dementia that can be treated under a doctor's care as it can exaggerate dementia symptoms. Depression usually responds well to treatment. (Mace & Rabins, 2019, p.154) These shifts, often abrupt and seemingly unfounded, stem from the brain's attempt to navigate its altered reality, a reality where the familiar becomes alien and the once stable ground of cognition shakes. Within this context, caregivers must operate from a code of empathy, recognizing that these behavioral tempests are not a reflection of choice but a manifestation of profound disorientation and fear experienced by their loved one. The courage required to face this aspect of dementia care is immense, a courage that draws not only from the well of personal fortitude but from the deeper springs of supernatural faith. In confronting these challenges, caregivers are often reminded of the biblical exhortation to find strength in weakness and to trust in the face of fear, embodying the paradox that true strength emerges from the acknowledgment of our weakness.

The DP may have a need or strong unmet request due to their inability to express it accurately, resulting in unpleasant emotions, as they are very frustrated at their inability to get through to you. This frustration can cause an abrupt downward mood swing. This requires you to be especially sensitive, alert, and aware of their body language and many other exterior factors to help you understand what they want. The clues are present; they just need a different set of "eyes" now. (Campbell, 2020) See Chapter 11.

The mysterious mood swings usually have nothing at all to do with you, it's just the damaged brain readjusting to try to adapt to unknown changes. It is common for the DP to falsely blame you or another caregiver for something or accuse you of stealing from them. Your DP is confused about where the misplaced item is. They have forgotten the location, and rather than ask you if you know its whereabouts, they go right to suspicion and skepticism. It is also common for the accused to react inappropriately with a strong defense and even an argument. This is an area where self-management is mandatory. Their stress or suspicion may not actually be about the item; it may be more about not being able to articulate what's needed. Arguing only escalates the stress. Instead, a good response would be to speak calmly and say, in short sentences, "Let's look for it together," or "Maybe it is in the _____." Then, wait a bit. "Do you want to go see?" etc. The DP may also not remember what a word or the questions mean. Try speaking a synonym or show the action with your hands and body, one step at a time. If it is more about not finding the right word, you can alleviate some frustration and offer a few different words to them. It is a relief for the DP to finally catch that unavailable term; if it comes through you, that is ok. Seek to understand them with kindness and gentleness with a double portion of self-control, which are a fruit of the spirit. We don't get some of the spiritual fruit, but all of it, which is why the word is not plural. This fruit is evidence of a maturing walk with Christ.

"But the fruit of the Spirit is love, joy, peace, longsuffering, kindness, goodness, faithfulness, gentleness, self-control. Against such, there is no law." - Galatians 5:22-23.

The DP has lost their footing, mentally, emotionally and physically. This is scary to the DP and they cannot clearly articulate it anymore. Be gentle with them, it must be horrifying to have pieces in their mind misfire or be unavailable. This requires a great deal of courage; courage is doing what one is scared to do, there can be no courage unless you're afraid. Whether they understand you or not, tell them you're so proud of them for being brave, and encourage them often.

"Let the weak say I am strong." - Joel 3:10

"My grace is sufficient for you, for My strength is made perfect in weakness." - II Cor. 12:9

"Whenever I am afraid I will trust in You." - Psalm 56:3.

8.2. The environment, both physical and emotional, in which care is provided plays a pivotal role in the management of dementia-related mood swings. Caregivers are thus tasked with the creation of a sanctuary that minimizes potential triggers of distress while promoting a sense of security and well-being. Adjustments may range from the tangible, such as the organization of living spaces to reduce confusion and the potential for frustration, to the intangible, such as the modulation of the caregiver's own emotional state and responses. The aim is to forge a setting where peace prevails, where the day's uncertainties are met with a steady calm that reassures and comforts. This endeavor, while challenging, is underpinned by the recognition that peace within creates peace without, a principle that guides the caregiver in their interactions and decision-making processes. If you've hidden God's word in your heart there will be an ample supply of peace to draw from. For your own well-being, practice the art of contentment by choosing forgiveness and gentleness as you understand the nature of dementia. We would not scold or force someone with cancer to get up and return to life as before. Be determined to forsake fretting as a habit. Like all unsavory habits, it needs to be replaced with a positive new way to correct the old habit. Consistently divert your anxiety to a favorite song and begin singing it quietly. Chains fall off when we sing praises to Him. Or try this technique; rub your fingertips together lightly and focus to become keenly aware of the sensations. (Chamine, 2016) Do this often to discipline your mind away from negative thinking. This kind of mindfulness can eventually take the sting out of a trigger which brings anger, frustration, or even hysterical yelling.

"Do not let any unwholesome talk come out of your mouths, but only what is helpful for building others up according to their needs, that it may benefit those who listen." - Ephesians 4:29

"Now godliness with contentment is great gain." - I Timothy 6:6

"Is anything too hard for the Lord?" - Genesis 18:14

8.3. A calming environment for one with dementia may be quite different from what the caregivers like, but it helps you, too. *"As a person who has dementia becomes upset, his ability to think and reason temporarily declines even more."* (Mace & Rabins, 2019, p. 32) This is true for anyone without dementia as well. When someone is very upset, highly charged and even hysterical, we too cannot think rationally in those moments. Realize this and find compassion and solutions for calm. The source of the real or imaginary distress must be investigated. If something isn't working, pivot. Then, after they are a bit calmer, start with a move to another location. In this action, they may forget entirely what they were so upset about. *Out of sight, out of mind may* work here. If the agitation sticks, learn not to force solutions but to temporarily let it go. If it's really a time issue, such as an appointment, maybe it wasn't meant to be on this particular day. Call for help to get them there if it is critically important. If they're in the wrong clothes (like pajamas) or won't bathe or eat first, learn to be prepared with a bag of clothes, wet wipes, food, etc., to take with you. Above all, keep yourself in peace and don't fret the small stuff. Try gently scratching the DP's head; it's calming and soothing, and look them in the eyes when speaking. Ask yourself, how important is it in light of eternity? Take the days in small steps, not wasting any valuable time with your loved one or being distracted by the inevitable cruel facts. Each day is precious, stay in the moment as the strain for the day is replaced with the strength for the day. (Fantasia, 2019)

"Therefore do not worry about tomorrow, for tomorrow will worry about its own things. Sufficient for the day is its own trouble." - Matthew 6:34

8.4 The importance of caregiver self-management during the DP's challenging behaviors. In the hard moments of these negative shifts in the DP's actions and attitude is the need for the caregiver's commitment to their own well-being. Their negative feelings can impact the DP's behavior in a circular motion. Even though these emotional offenses accidentally cause you real pain, anger, or frustration, be confident to know that they are (frequently) not on purpose. They stem from brain damage and not the soul of your loved one. Recognize your feelings and put them in the context of a disease doing the slight, not your DP. Rather than *roll with the punches*, realize the punches are a shadow; thus, arguing or retaliation is foolish and futile.

Go get a cup of tea and refill your proverbial emotional cup, too. The adage that one cannot pour from an empty cup finds weighty relevance here, as the demands of caregiving can exhaust one's reserves of patience, empathy, and strength. Take a break, recognize the fruit of self-control is needed again, pray for gratitude, and ask Jesus to activate it.

Techniques such as breathing exercises, which invite moments of pause and restoration, and the practice of detachment, where one learns to separate the person from their illness, become invaluable tools. Detachment means a way of emotionally separating the challenging behaviors from the soul of the person you love and care for. It can also mean for you to detach emotionally from the offense. Remember to be like a thermostat that gets set on a temperature and not a thermometer that changes temperature with its surroundings. That sort of behavior is called codependency; it can sabotage your relationships as well as be a severe detriment to your own well-being. If you are too enmeshed with your DP or anyone else, I suggest you read a book or blog on codependency; Melody Beatty is the best author on this subject. This can help in every area of your life.

These practices not only mitigate the stress experienced by the caregiver but, by modeling calm and control, serve to stabilize the environment, benefiting both the caregiver and care recipient. Repeat it often; don't take it personally; it's the disease talking or doing!

"You will keep him in perfect peace, whose mind is stayed on You because he trusts in You." - Isaiah 26:3.

"A soft answer turns away wrath, but a harsh word stirs up anger." - Proverbs 15:1

8.5 Common signs of stress in caregivers and why managing stress is crucial for both caregivers and those they care for. The relentless nature of dementia caregiving can insidiously erode the caregiver's resilience, manifesting in symptoms of stress that, if left unaddressed, can have damaging effects on both the caregiver and the quality of care provided. Acknowledging the signs of stress, from physical fatigue to emotional despondency, is the first step towards mitigating its impact. I will say this several times as it is of utmost importance: establishing connections with individuals or groups who share the caregiving journey can provide not only practical support and advice but also a sense of community and understanding that alleviates the isolation often felt in this role. Whether found in the tangible spheres of support groups or online forums, this network is a vital resource, offering solace and strength drawn from shared experience and collective wisdom. I also highly recommend family members, near or far, join their own dementia support group to gain familiarity with the enormous job a caregiver has and learn ways to relieve some of the stress.

You must find and establish at least two loyal relationships with people you can relate to because they are either on the same path, further along, or have been there before and are now without their DP. These people have a much-needed perspective and practical life skills for you to learn about and possibly use yourself. They can be found online, as a support group for dementia, at a community center, or in a church / temple group, etc. A few easy internet searches or an inquiry on the Dementia/Alzheimer's Facebook group can bring results. It's best to seek these contacts early rather than when you're exhausted or depleted. If the first person or group is not a good fit, keep looking and don't give up. As you do, seek direction from God for your new friend(s). When it's right, they will be more than happy to help you, advise you, and bring much-needed camaraderie. Though they will not replace your internal compass, they may just be there to listen.

"Do not be conformed to this world, but be transformed by the renewal of your mind, that by testing you may discern what is the good and acceptable and perfect will of God." - Romans 12:2.

8.6 Mindfulness (situational awareness) and biblical meditation can be powerful tools for stress management, present-moment awareness, and self-control. In the silent moments before dawn, when the world lies hushed and expectations for the day ahead are yet unformed, caregivers often find themselves in a reflective pause. It is in these quiet hours that the weight of their role is both a burden and a calling, a sacred trust that demands more than physical stamina—it requires a wellspring of spiritual strength. If at all possible, cultivate a few moments of mindfulness and biblical meditations to fill your emotional tank for the day's duties. The practices of mindfulness and biblical meditation offer a refuge from the storm, a means to anchor the soul amidst the tempest of caregiving. These disciplines invite a shift in perspective, a focus of the mind on the present moment and on the immutable truths of faith that provide solace and strength. Through meditation on scripture, caregivers are reminded of the constancy of divine love and the promise of strength in weakness, insights that illuminate the path forward with hope and clarity. This spiritual grounding fosters a resilience that enables caregivers to meet each day's challenges not with trepidation but with a heart steadied by faith and a spirit imbued with power. Deliberately being in a mind of repose can rebuild and restore one's ability to calmly respond, not react, to the DP's irritating or unnecessary behaviors. In a later chapter, I will touch on the importance of good sleep.

"Blessed is the man who walks not in the counsel of the ungodly, nor stands in the path of sinners, nor sits in the seat of the scornful, but his delight is in the law of the Lord, and in His law he meditates day and night. He shall be like a tree planted by the rivers of water, that brings

forth its fruit in its season, whose leaf also shall not wither; and whatever he does shall prosper." - Psalm 1: 1-3.6

8.7. Balancing caregiving responsibilities with the need for personal time to attend to one's own health and well-being. Self-care is the fulcrum upon which caregiving balances it is an act of self-preservation that permits sustained support for the loved one. This balance is not found but forged through deliberate choices and conscious allocation of time and energy. It necessitates an acknowledgment that the caregiver's needs hold equal merit to those of the person they care for, deserving of time, attention, and action. Caregiver needs must be added to the schedule, not to be relinquished to a remote possibility. Creating boundaries within which self-care can flourish involves not only the demarcation of time for such activities but also the cultivation of an environment in which these practices are respected and upheld. Within these boundaries, the caregiver can find respite and rejuvenation, drawing upon the strength garnered to return to their role with renewed vigor and compassion.

"I am the vine, you are the branches. He who abides in Me, and I in him, bears much fruit; for without Me you can do nothing." - John 15:5

8.8 Harmony, adaptability and flexibility are necessary. There may be a lot of moving parts in this role as a dementia person's caregiver. It is best that you adopt a manner of teachability rather than stubbornly do everything the same as you always had. There is wisdom to know what needs to change and what does not. Release control over to God and His resources that are brought to you or those you've carefully sought out. After all, you did not cause this disease, nor can you cure it, or control it. So it is futile to try, but is not futile to help and care for your DP. In this attitude of acceptance and surrender of absolute control, you will discover a peace that passes understanding and even joy in the journey that gives you the strength to go forward. Since the DP is changing, being rigid may break them, in a sense. There is peace in surrendering to a new way of life, rather than forcing old habits.

"And no one puts new wine into old wineskins. For the old skins would burst from the pressure, spilling the wine and ruining the skins. New wine is stored in new wineskins so that both are preserved." - Matthew 9:17

"So Jesus said to them who believed him, "If you abide in my word, you are truly my disciples, and you will know the truth, and the truth will set you free." - John 8:31-32

8.9. The unpredictability inherent in dementia care often renders rigid schedules untenable, necessitating a flexible approach that prioritizes essential tasks while allowing for the fluctuations of the care recipient's needs and moods. This flexibility, grounded in a commitment to present-focused care, enables caregivers to adapt to the day's demands with grace and efficacy. The establishment of routines that accommodate both the caregiver's and the care recipient's needs foster a rhythm to daily life that mitigates stress and enhances the quality of care, embodying the scriptural principle of committing one's work to the Lord to establish one's plans. A daily planner and a medication log are for you both, not just the DP. Frivolous distractions and unexpected interruptions can spoil time management. Though some interruptions are good and beneficial and ought to be valued and welcomed. Be discerning and keenly aware of the time to stay the course as much as possible, but do not hold it with an iron fist.

"Commit to the Lord whatever you do, and he will establish your plans." - Proverbs 16:3

"Then those who fear the Lord spoke to one another, and the Lord listened and heard them; so a book of remembrance was written before Him for those who fear the Lord and who meditate on His name." - Malachi 3:16

9

NUTRITIONAL NEEDS, FEEDING CHALLENGES AND A GARDEN

Dementia can affect appetite; here, you'll find strategies to address these changes. To meet nutritional needs, creating colorful, appealing, nutritious, yet easy-to-handle meals may be necessary. Your DP may no longer remember what they enjoy eating, or, at times, they may have forgotten that they just ate and ask for food. As with a child, it is critical to avoid indulging them with empty-calorie food to keep the peace. Mealtime can be difficult when the DP stubbornly refuses to eat what is served. This, too, requires you to be a sensitive investigator as you seek the root cause. It may be that the food upsets them because they don't remember how to use a fork or spoon. Or maybe they have a stomachache, toothache, or other pain. All kinds of reasons could be the culprit. If it's not discovered, I suggest you put the food in the refrigerator and let time and hunger overrule their resistance. As with most beings, they'll eat when they're hungry enough or when the next meal is served. If they refuse all food, it sounds like time to speak to the doctor.

Furthermore, being creative comes in handy with meal preparation. Include different textures and colors in your food if your DP appreciates variety. However, if they refuse new things, go back to their favorites. Since their long-term memory is more intact, serve their favorite familiar meals for less resistance. To keep confusion at bay, do not put many options in front of them all at once. Serve them **one** protein, starch, and vegetable **at a time**; you may want to start with the vegetable. Be responsible for seasoning it, as this could ruin the food if salt & pepper are left on the table and accidentally overused. Your support group or online recipe sites can share their ideas for attractive and nutritious meals. If the food looks good, is small enough to pick up with their fingers, and is good, it will be easier for you both. In the latter stages of dementia, they will usually need personal help to eat.

If, for whatever reason, cooking and cleaning up every night has become too difficult, some very good options for healthy, affordable, prepackaged meals are available at stores like Florida's **Ideal Nutrition** (idealnutritionnow.com).

Other options in the US are **Factor,** (Factor75.com) **Fresh N Lean,** (freshnlean.com) **Cook Unity,** (cookunity.com) **Freshly,** (freshly.com) and **Snap Kitchen** (snapkitchen.com). Many will deliver if they have a shop in your area.

Further options are freshly packaged meals from stores like:

Whole Foods, Sprouts Farmers Market, The Fresh Market, Harris Teeter, Gelson's Market Kitchen, Shaw's, Wegmans Cafe, Meijer, Safeway, Market Basket & Trader Joe's.

I suggest careful consideration to rule out excessive salt, sugar and fat content from stores, especially the last several ones listed here.

"Beloved, I pray that all may go well with you and that you may be in good health, as it goes well with your soul." - III John: 1:2

9.2. Strategies for social events such as friends' homes, restaurants, weddings, family picnics, etc., and how to know when this is no longer possible. In the earlier stages, many DP's are fine at a social gathering or may become very introverted, shy, or fearful as they are somewhat aware of their memory loss. A friend's home is probably the easiest for them to attend, but you will still need to remain close to them for comfort and answers.

Often, large gatherings are too much for the DP; they are overwhelmed and may let off steam inappropriately. They are fearful of having to talk to others as this skill is fading; they don't want to be confused or embarrassed in public. Neither do they want to be shamed or humiliated, discernment is critical when bringing the DP to these events. Eating out may very well be a thing of the past when your DP shows an elevated amount of irritability, rude behaviors, wandering, or unreasonableness to cooperate so all can enjoy the time together. Your DP is not deliberately being rude, it is just that the deep levels of their mind have now been scrambled and inappropriate thoughts have risen to the top and released. The filter that held etiquette, politeness and self-control is damaged or will be gone altogether. If they refuse to sit quietly, so as to not disturb other patrons, or eat the food presented to them, it may be time to keep the DP at home, where things are always more familiar. These behaviors are indicators that the DP is miscalculating the situation or the person(s). It may also be that something else is awry. If this occurs, you will need sensitivity to discover what is going on and stay close by to reassure them over and over, speaking gentle reminders (who, where, what, how, etc.) when someone speaks to them and use physical touch to comfort and direct them.

If there is a big event coming that you want to attend with your DP, start with a small dinner out at a familiar place before you decide to take them to a wedding, for example. Even then, assign a few people the DP is comfortable with, to take turns to sit with them and be flexible to leave early if necessary. As with anyone, it is insulting to talk about the DP when they are present and can hear what you are saying unless it's basic instructions or introductions. An easy tip from the Alzheimer's Association to notify the staff of their situation by producing a simple business card that concisely explains the condition to alleviate any concerns. This can be done and printed from a home computer. The card can be indiscreetly handed to anyone working near the DP. You can also let the manager know.

If your DP is in the early stage, and you want to take them to an outdoor event like a picnic or concert, you will need some extra security measures and a keen awareness of how much stimulation they can tolerate and remain calm. Have at least one other person of the same sex as your DP, to go along and take them to the bathroom. Two or more trustworthy people are better so you can delegate teams for a safety net. You will want this safety net of extra sets of eyes so you too can enjoy the setting. It is unwise to expect the DP to remember all the same rules for personal safety they once knew. Even if your person with dementia is not known for wandering, it can occur suddenly. Be prepared and be alert.

"Be sober, be vigilant; because your adversary the devil walks about like a roaring lion, seeking whom he may devour." - I Peter 5:8

"Behold, I give you the authority to trample on serpents and scorpions, and over all the power of the enemy, and nothing shall by any means hurt you." - Luke 10:19

9.3. Tips to ensure adequate hydration, encourage fluid intake and maintain cleanliness for staying healthy. Try a simple thing like buying your DP a new adult travel cup with a lid and place for a straw that would appeal to them. Practice keeping your cup filled with water and fill theirs too. Hydration can eliminate headaches and fatigue. Bladder leakage may become a problem, so be aware of this, especially if it was already an issue before dementia. Having enough fluid intake is an essential preventative measure to ensure urinary tract health and keep the bowels moving. Avoid drinks with a lot of caffeine, as it can cause dehydration.

Your DP may need reminding and help with simple things we take for granted, like how to use toilet paper, flush, and wash their hands, as these memories decline. Keep a package of fresh wipes around the home for any accidental messes. Extra diligence in the bathroom keeps everyone healthier. Body wipes don't get all the invisible bacteria, though they are better than nothing. If you are near a bidet, have them use it. Or if there's a handheld shower, it's worth the extra effort to use this often after a bathroom visit. It's one extra step, but it does a better job of eradicating E. coli and other bacteria. A urinary tract infection, UTI, is more common in women than men. Taking antibiotics to cure a UTI has side effects that are not pleasant, and overuse of them may make the bacteria resistant to their effectiveness. A UTI can also heighten dementia symptoms and even mimic them in someone without dementia. Doctors will tell you that this is one of those medications that may aggravate cognition. (Mace & Rabins, 2011) Additionally, the DP may not be able to tell you their symptoms and get the medical help needed, becoming very irritable without evidentiary reasons. An ounce of prevention **is** worth a pound of cure.

"Therefore, whether you eat or drink, or whatever you do, do all to the glory of God." - I Corinthians 10:31

"He who believes in Me, as the Scripture has said, out of his heart will flow rivers of living water." - John 7:38

9.4. Maintaining a balanced diet that supports energy levels and overall health. The sustenance that fuels the DP and the caregiver's body is as much a foundation of care as the most tender gesture or attentive task. Nutrition, balanced and intentional, supports not only the physical demands placed upon the caregiver but also serves as a bulwark against the tide of stress, fatigue, and illness. The endeavor to maintain a diet that nourishes requires both foresight and simplicity—planning meals or purchasing precooked meals that are both nutritious and uncomplicated ensures that the act of eating nurtures rather than burdens. Incorporating whole and fresh foods, rich in vitamins, minerals, and other essential nutrients, fortifies the caregiver's and the DP's health, providing the stamina necessary to navigate the complexities of care as well as keeping both the DP's and your immune systems in top function. Being a caregiver is already highly stressful; we must avoid exacerbating this by indulging in habitual unhealthy habits. If the caregiver becomes ill, it can significantly impact the emotional and physical well-being of the person with dementia if you are not able to be there for them.

"Do not be wise in your own eyes; fear the Lord and depart from evil. It will be health to your flesh and strength to your bones." - Proverbs 3:7-8.

9.5. Gardening is a powerful and beneficial idea for the DP in early to mid-stage dementia. The idea is for the caregiver and the DP, along with others to build, plant, irrigate, fertilize, weed, and harvest a small, manageable-sized raised bed to grow vegetables and ground fruit, like strawberries or a blueberry bush, depending on climate. This idea has several benefits, including enlisting help from the DP, which builds their self-esteem. It also has the added value of producing food. I have seen the DP become quite taken with this idea and is very happy with the first plant that goes on the dinner plate. It's for those who are in a climate or season to support this and have the ground and/or permission to use it. This task may involve several people to design and set up the garden near a water source. Use materials like untreated wood, stone, or recycled plastic for the structure. Ensure the beds have good drainage by drilling holes or elevating them slightly if necessary. Add tennis-ball size rocks or larger sticks on the bottom, then use a mix of *high-quality* garden soil, compost, and organic matter plus some of the available local dirt to mix in. Lay out a grid to separate the types and sizes of plants. To protect it from bunnies, squirrels, etc., you may need a chicken wire dome over it or just around the perimeter. Ask experienced neighbors or a gardening center for tips and directions on what and when to plant in your specific area. If funds aren't there, seek help from your support group and/or family. The act of planting seeds or seedlings, caring for them, and watching them grow is very therapeutic for all. Consider if this undertaking is feasible for your situation and loca-tion. If it is not, modify the idea with a small porch garden, a single pot with a cage for tomatoes or a few potted herbs by the window for cooking. Either way, get the DP involved if they can still partic-ipate. The hard work and care that goes into setting this up is amply rewarded.

"Do not be deceived, God is not mocked; for whatever a man sows, that he will also reap." - Galatians 6:7.

"He shall be like a tree planted by the rivers of water, that brings forth its fruit in its season, whose leaf also shall not wither; and whatever he does shall prosper." - Psalm 1:3

9.6. Malnutrition is common in dementia people, especially if they live alone or are in a nursing home. If your DP is in a facility, you are their advocate to ensure proper nutritional care. If the DP insists on living alone, you must recognize the signs that they can no longer live this way for many reasons. See Chapter 21. Their freedom is something they may want to preserve at any cost, but remember, they are not able to think rationally enough to make a sound and safe decision. Poor nutrition leads to many avoidable, additional health and dental problems. Neither of you wants these added burdens.

Your DP needs assistance in choosing healthy food that is fresh, easy to eat, and readily available; see above in this Chapter. They may need you to cut it into easier to chew bite sizes. If they are not eating well regularly and have lost weight, let them have healthy snacks at will. If they can eat nuts, leave unshelled walnuts, pistachios, pumpkin seed nuts, etc. out. Leave Rubbermaid-style closed tubs or zip lock-style bags with food such as: cut up cheese, mixed tuna or chopped meat, cut vegetables: peas, carrots or cucumbers, etc., fresh chunks of watermelon, cantaloupe, avocado, or hard-boiled eggs in the fridge for them to get. Make sure that you are around whenever they eat or get an alarm for the refrigerator to be aware of choking possibilities with harder foods. If you are not skilled with the Heimlich: Abdominal Thrust maneuver for choking, please learn this oft life-saving tactic. Also, have small containers of yogurt, humus, pudding, or applesauce available too.

Other sources of supplements are available in liquid form, such as **Ensure, Boost, Glucerna, Huel,** or **Kirkland brand from Costco,** etc. They are expensive and need not become a habit. I suggest you do **not** swap them for a meal unless entirely necessary and only for a short time and convenience. Consider them a "milkshake" for your DP, not a meal. They can have unpleasant side effects, such as gastrointestinal issues like diarrhea, bloating, and constipation. Furthermore, these may lack fiber, certain vitamins and minerals, and contain too much sugar. Many have artificial ingredients as well.

In the shadowed corners of caregiving, where stress and exhaustion converge, the allure of quick fixes and immediate comforts beckons. The draw of alcohol or unhealthy foods as salves for the weary soul is potent, promising solace but delivering consequences that compound the burdens borne. Vigilance against these temptations requires awareness of their detrimental effects and cultivating healthier coping mechanisms. Substituting these fleeting comforts with activities that nourish both body and mind —engaging in physical activity, seeking solace in nature, or connecting with supportive peers—can redirect the caregiver's path towards wellness rather than further strain. Allowing any kind of alcohol consumption for the DP is a dangerous step toward the unknown. They will not tolerate a beer or a mixed drink like before, as it may result in them getting extra dizzy, obnoxious, or delusional. It is just not a smart idea to add fire to the kindling. They have a hard enough time dealing with this novel life completely sober. Furthermore, most medications should not be mixed with alcohol, or the drink may destroy their efficacy. No matter how much they ask to have a drink, it is in their best interest that all alcohol is off limits, especially after the initial stage of dementia. If it is out of sight, it may also stay out of mind. If there is any alcohol in the home, it is wise to keep it unseen and unavailable.

This conscious choice to avoid the immediate for the beneficial underscores the caregiver's commitment to your health and that of the DP, too. Drinking can also undermine the longevity and capacity of your caregiving. Nevertheless, this doesn't mean that a beer or a glass of wine for you is off-limits entirely, as long as it does not become a habit or a necessity.

If you are dealing with a DP who is or was alcohol dependent, that requires a whole different set of solutions and strategies. Like dementia, untreated alcoholism ends in insanity and or death.

"Do not look on the wine when it is red, when it sparkles in the cup, when it swirls around smoothly; At the last it bites like a serpent, and stings like a viper. Your eyes will see strange things, and your heart will utter perverse things." - Proverbs 23:31-33

QUALITY REJUVENATING SLEEP

Quality sleep, including non-medical strategies to improve falling to sleep and staying there. The sanctity of sleep, often besieged by the relentless pace and emotional weight of caregiving, demands vigilant protection. Quality rest, the cornerstone of mental acuity and emotional stability, often eludes those who find themselves perpetually attuned to the needs and nuances of another. Your DP may have night episodes of wandering, getting lost in the dark, or seeking food or drink. They may have a different circadian rhythm than they used to; it's often one's age or the dementia brain making these changes. Try to keep them awake all day to avoid nighttime interruptions. Naps are so comforting, but you may pay for them overnight. If they awaken, they may need your gentle reassurance of where they are and that all is well. Or maybe they just need a trip to the bathroom, so keep the nightlight on in this area of the home for you both. See Chapter 21.

Medications taken in the daytime may contribute to their drowsiness or the opposite as well. Be very cautious using evening sedatives as they can have symptoms that may be worse than being awakened. (See Chapter 19) This is an area for your physician(s) to consider. The natural way is best for their overall health. Look for products that include the minerals and herbs, magnesium, melatonin, GABA, L-theanine, ashwagandha, valerian root and L-tryptophan, such as **Relaxium**. Others to consider are: **Nature's Bounty Sleep3, Nested Naturals Luna, Dr. Emil Nutrition 5-HTP Plus, Zhou Driftoff,** or **Onnit New Mood, etc.**

A few practices that help include establishing a pre-sleep ritual that signals the body and mind to wind down. Be creative in establishing a calming evening routine to help mitigate any reluctance to go to bed. Through your actions, you are reaffirming the value of each moment spent in the company of your DP, as these days are shortening. First, optimize the sleep environment by making it cool, dark, and quiet. To relax and even promote sleep, set the lighting to dim and give and receive a comforting back rub and/or foot rub. Scratching the head or combing the hair is a simple yet calming way to relieve some of the agitation symptoms and show love at the same time. Once in bed, a tried-and-true technique is to utilize your own white noise device or "Relaxing White Noise" on YouTube, which can filter out distractions as well as send soothing messages to the brain. There is scientific evidence that these kinds of sounds are cathartic for those who struggle with sleep issues. There are other "colored" noises that have a different effect on the brain to promote deep sleep. Brown, green or pink noises have positive results for falling asleep and staying there. Of course, sounds are not in color, but the style of sound is labeled with a color to differentiate them. Try different ones and see what your DP responds to. You may also want to try nature sounds, such as ocean waves, raindrop sounds, birds softly chirping, or a crackling fire, etc. If any of these are unsuccessful or ineffective, try a box or floor fan; it may indeed help with the sound as well as the breeze.

"Because you have made the Lord, who is my refuge, even the Most High, your dwelling place, no evil shall befall you, nor shall any plague come near your dwelling; for He shall give His angels charge over you, to keep you in all your ways." Psalm 91:9-11 "I lay down and slept; I awoke, for the Lord sustained me." - Psalm 3:5

"When you lie down, you will not be afraid; Yes, you will lie down and your sleep will be sweet." - Proverbs 3:24

10.2. Everyone, including the DP, gets a better night's sleep if they exercise for at least 30 minutes that day. If you cannot exercise with them on any particular day, it is best for you to delegate this. Most adult daycare centers are great sources for your DP's physical well-being, as it is regularly scheduled. See Chapter 20. Caregiver stress may torment you at night with circulating thoughts that keep you awake. The technique mentioned earlier from Shirzad Chamine's Positive Intelligence can help here. He calls it our PQ, or positive intelligence quotient. (Chamine, 2016) Though it sounds simple or silly this activity will redirect your left-hemisphere survival brain away from the incessant sabotage thoughts and into the right-hemisphere brain of calm emotions, creativity, and peace. Pray first, then lightly rub your fingertips together and keenly concentrate on the sensations. You can use your fingertips on the sheets next. Doing this laser-focus action will take the attention off your internal dialog and shift to calm. Then listen intently, deliberately to the white noise until you fall asleep. Do the PQ detail often anytime repetitive thinking gets in the way of your daytime peace or nighttime sleep. After 21 days, it has become a habit, and it works faster. Depending on the stage your DP is in, the PQ technique may be too lofty for them to acquire and stay with consistently, but it can work well for you.

Another thing is to keep a pad of paper near you and scribble down any thoughts or ideas that keep coming to you. The point is

to put them on paper and out of your mind, they may be important to save and help you in the morning.

Deep sleep becomes a mission of utmost importance, ensuring that
the caregiver awakens refreshed and ready to face the challenges
of a new day.

*"I will both lie down in peace, and sleep; For You alone, O Lord, make me
dwell in safety."* - Psalm 4:8

*"And let the beauty of the Lord our God be upon us and establish the
work of our hands for us; yes, establish the work of our hands.* - Psalm
90:17.

THE IMPORTANCE OF ROUTINE IN CREATING A SAFE SPACE

The benefits of maintaining a daily routine for individuals with dementia include reduced confusion and increased security. Include daily, weekly, and monthly criteria as well as specific medical appointments. As a side note: if you take the DP to an appointment and stop at a store, it might be wise to check their pockets before you leave. Since they have forgotten norms and rules, they may see something they want and pocket it. Calmly take them to the check-out and pay for the item if it's something small like a candy bar or gum. If it's a watch or a piece of jewelry kind of item, try to let them know what good taste they have but take them back to that area and "shop" for this together. During this episode, try to distract them or use a fib and glibly say, "Let's go to _____. They have a better selection." Once in the car they'll have most likely forgotten. In the future, make it a point to casually look in their pockets or purse for an array of "treasures." Be warned, some of these may be organic in nature.

Your DP needs to keep a daily routine as much as possible. To prevent a disruption that can cause a mood swing, both positive and/or negative, I strongly recommend you make it clear to family, friends, and neighbors not to drop by unannounced. Install a video doorbell such as a RING or WYZE device (discussed more in a later chapter). For those who do stop by unannounced, create a sign at the door that says something like, "An appointment is kindly requested", as you must think of the DP first. If they're dropping off food etc., ask that they text or email you or the respite caregiver to receive the item(s). Put a cooler with a lock on the porch, stoop, or garage to receive the food when you are unable to get to the door. Still, there may be a time when the visitor has caught you both at a good time and is welcome to come in. In this way, you can be flexible with the routine, but do tell the visitor up front how much time you have and deliberately look at the clock or watch when the time is close.

"Let brotherly love continue. Do not forget to entertain strangers, for by so doing some have unwittingly entertained angels." - Hebrews 13:1-2

11.2. In the intricate web of caregiving, the physical environment takes on a pivotal role, necessitating meticulous scrutiny to preempt the commonplace hazards that may lurk within the seemingly benign confines of a home. Initiating this evaluation, one might first turn their gaze towards the floors, seeking out any obstructions or uneven surfaces that whisper promises of falls, the most treacherous of foes for the DP or the elderly. The journey continues with a vigilant eye cast towards securing rugs, ensuring they lie flat and firm against the floor, bound by non-slip underlays that defy the attempts of shifting feet to displace them. If they are loose at all, they must go. If they cover loose flooring, it must be secured.

In the atmosphere of lighting where shadows cast by inadequate illumination become specters of confusion, disorientation, and fear. Here, the installation of motion-sensor lights, especially near exit doors, emerges as a beacon of safety, their luminescence guiding paths through the darkness. Several bright night lights should suffice in most areas. The expedition for safety does not halt at the physical but extends its reach into domestic chemicals, where medications and cleaning agents, once benign, transform into potential sources of harm. These agents must be sequestered, relegated to areas beyond reach, or locked away, inaccessible to anyone but you or your respite. Preemptive care weaves its way through the home, from the barricades placed at stairwells to the alarms positioned at doors. Another preemptive effort is to cover their favorite seats with waterproof pads or even the entire furniture with vinyl for easy cleaning. This keeps it clean and dry and keeps it in good condition.

"Your word is a lamp to my feet and a light to my path." - Psalm 119:105

11.3. Structuring the day for success and stability helps everyone. Tips for creating a routine that accommodates the unique needs of someone with dementia. In the DP's world, almost everything is different and unstable. It makes perfect sense to try to keep routines as consistent as possible so we don't add to their stress and anxiety. Even though they'll forget much along the way, it is best not to test their flexibility with any unnecessary changes unless they are truly needed. The routine should be as similar as possible to the daily living tasks they were used to for many years. Daily routines bring relaxation and security when the DP certainly needs this. See Chapter 17 on Activities of Daily Life.

"Let all things be done decently and in order." - I Corinthians 14:40 II Cor. 12:9a

11.4. Include their favorite fun times in the routine as well as the caregiver's preferences, if at all possible. One idea is to sort through old photographs by years and maybe by travel vacations, old homes, or cars. The trips may be recalled in part and most of us find vacations a fun and happy memory. But if your DP cannot recall at all, skip them altogether or for another time.

These reminiscing strategies can bring both happy times and a baffling, frustrating absence of any memory at all. It's best to move on and not try to dislodge the answer to who's in the photograph. If they give a wrong answer to who the person is, smile and say something affirming rather than corrective. Then skip to the people they already identified and talk about them. Try not to start a question with, "Remember when we?" or "Remember when?". These remember questions may result in a mood change and not for the better. Just keep your remarks to, "That was a fun time" or "I like her dress, do you?" Speak in first-person narrative and be sensitive to their lack of recall.

"I will remember the deeds of the Lord; yes, I will remember your miracles of long ago." - Psalm 77:11

"I thank my God every time I remember you." - Phillipians 1:3

11.5. Mastering non-verbal cues for better understanding is detective work. It is important to observe and attempt to interpret body language and facial expressions of those with dementia to improve understanding and connection. Facial expressions do not necessarily indicate a physical problem; many times, they are the result of the DP's internal struggle with understanding the situation and their frustration with their lack of recall. They can also often be humiliated by themselves. Envelop them with a large dose of compassion and grace.

Instead of words, there are simple ways to teach your DP with hand motions to ask to go to the bathroom, that they're hungry or thirsty, and other requests. DPs often have incontinence issues, so it's important to let them go as quickly and as often as possible, and in later stages, they may need help with undressing. Hydration is critical for health and preventing infection, though it does mean more bathroom breaks. These hand motions are to be created by you and will be unique to your DP. They may change or be too confusing for you both as the decline of dementia progresses. Some caregivers have created a portable chart with sticker pictures for the DP to point to. They work best in the early stages. Later, these charts can get thrown across the room in frustration, so be aware they are not perfect tools.

The power of a gentle, reassuring touch is a form of communication and connection. There will be times when verbal communication is either ineffective or incapable. Just a warm touch to direct them, soothe them, or to offer sympathy, etc., can be a powerful gesture that the DP will usually appreciate.

"Love does no wrong to a neighbor; therefore love is the fulfillment of the law." - Romans 13:10

"Love is patient, love is kind and is not jealous; love does not brag and is not arrogant." - 1 Corinthians 13:4

LEVERAGING MUSIC AND ART: NON-VERBAL COMMUNICATION

Music therapy is significant for memory recall and emotional expression. While listening to music, every area of the brain is activated! Turn on their favorite songs especially when life is getting stressful or dull and depressed. It may very well eliminate a decline in mood or attitude. Familiar soothing music can bring tranquility, upbeat rhythmic music may initiate their movement, or even some sweet melodic memories are positively triggered by certain songs. According to Martin Luther King Jr., a good song becomes a "backdoor key to unlock the mind". It may quickly initiate smiling and even dancing, which is great, beneficial exercise! The language of music transcends words or melodies, it is a powerful weapon to cast away fear, doubt, anger, sadness, etc. Music is also one of those long-term memories that are slow to fade. Singer-songwriter Glen Campbell could still perform his songs well into his Alzheimer's diagnosis. (Campbell, 2020) He remembered the words and could play the guitar nearly as well as he could 20 years before. His music was a muscle memory that was slow to decline. It brought everyone joy to see and was one thing that was still available to him for quite a while. Seeing your DP's face light up when an old familiar song is played will be joyful.

"God inhabits the praises of His people" - Psalm 22:3

*"When the trumpeters and singers were as one, to make one sound to be heard in praising and thanking the Lord, and when they lifted up their voice with the trumpets, cymbals and instruments of **music**, and praised the Lord, saying: "For He is good, For His mercy endures forever," that the house, the house of the Lord, was filled with a cloud,"* - II Chronicles 5:13

12.2. Practical advice on incorporating music into the care plan. I strongly urge you, the caregiver, to watch the documentary on dementia, "Alive Inside". You will see amazing responses to the late-stage DP hearing their own decades of music on headphones. The one treating the DP says that "music can activate more parts of the brain than any other stimulation". (Alive Inside) We are taught in this documentary that "music can heal trauma, stimulate lucidity, and emotions."(Alive Inside) It is clear to see that memory and physical movement (dance) are activated. It's quite a delightful and surprising scene for the DP and for all to witness.

Use your CD's or a vinyl record player. You can ask **Amazon Alexa, Google Nest, or Apple HomePod** to play music. First, set up one or more music platform accounts like:

Spotify, Pandora, Soundcloud, iHeart Radio, Google Play, Tidal, Deezer, Apple, Amazon, or YouTube Music to play all your favorites.

All decades of music are readily available on digital demand by simply speaking it out loud. Ask a tech-savvy person how to set this device up if needed. Help the DP put on a pair of headphones or wireless earbuds and watch them come *alive inside*! Put your own set on to help you take away the stress of the day and transport you back to a happier, more free time in your life. You may wind up dancing together, which is great exercise and lots of fun.

"Let our master now command your servants, who are before you, to seek out a man who is a skillful player on the harp. And it shall be that he will play it with his hand when the distressing spirit from God is upon you, and you shall be well." - I Samuel 16:16.

"Finally, my brethren, be strong in the Lord and in the power of His might." - Ephesians 6:10.

12.3. How visual art activities can provide a means of expression and emotional release for individuals with dementia. Depending on their level of ability, discuss what kinds of art expression the dementia person can participate in by actually creating it or observing what someone else has created. Music can be a backdrop during tactile art, or the focal point to calm the nervous system and relax the body to be more receptive to cooperation.

If they used to paint, draw, or use another medium, an attempt at this activity may be worth it before the ability is erased altogether. God purposefully gives individuals gifts or talents to serve others and beautify and glorify His creation. Some gifts can reach the DP, whereas other means will not. Art is always subjective; what the DP may find beautiful or soothing is not necessarily your taste. Their tastes may have even changed with the onset of dementia and may change again.

"Every good gift and every perfect gift is from above and comes down from the Father of lights, with whom there is no variation or shadow of turning." - James 1:17

"And I have filled him with the Spirit of God, in wisdom, in understanding, in knowledge, and in all manner of workmanship, to design artistic works, to work in gold, in silver, in bronze, in cutting jewels for setting, in

carving wood, and to work in all manner of workmanship." - Exodus 31:3-5

12.4. The importance of sensory engagement and its positive effects on well-being. Often the senses are not entirely damaged by the disease all at once. By trial and error, find the senses the patient still has control of and utilize these. Keep the focus off the dormant senses. If all six senses are still available, engaging them all is a blessing. Nature is a fantastic way to identify which senses are still viable and to stimulate them. Outdoors, in a park or a garden, by a lake, or at the ocean, can bring many senses to mind as they can calm and comfort a restless soul. It is especially beneficial for both of you to allow fresh air and a change in atmosphere, whenever possible.

I have a smell memory of the scent of smoking a pipe. It is a smoky cherry tobacco smell, and if I ever encounter this, I immediately am brought back to a vivid and happy scene with my father, who loved to smoke this kind of pipe tobacco. It is a fact that the olfactory nerves have a unique ability to instantly bring a pleasant emotional memory in its vivid setting. Our sense of smell can change a person's mood and mind quite fast. It is a clever way to indirectly help in times of emotional weakness for both the DP and the caregiver. Identify their favorite scents and try to keep the aromas in the DP's favorite places in the home. Scented oils, cologne, or perfume do the job well.

"The heavens declare the glory of God, and the firmament shows His handiwork." - Psalm 19:1.

13

PRAYER AND PEACE ALONG THE JOURNEY

We may already know that "The effectual fervent prayer of a righteous person avails much," from James 5:16 and it is true that dealing with dementia can certainly make our prayers fervent. Personal prayer is our source of strength and solace for Christian caregivers and the DP. If the DP is willing and has faith, they can be included in team prayers. Praying out loud together is a bonding experience and may have been a habit from before dementia appeared. How comforting to know that *"Wherever two or three are gathered together in My name, I am there in the midst of them."* - Matthew 18:20

As the disease progresses, be mindful that this may need to change or be eliminated as a duo so that you can stay focused and undistracted on your own relationship with the Lord. Praying out loud speaks volumes to the supernatural for changes in the natural. As you seek the Lord in prayer, pray His promises, not only your pain.

As He said, "Without faith it is impossible to please Him." - Hebrews 11:6

"Continue earnestly in prayer, being vigilant in it with thanksgiving;" - Colossians 4:2

"Out of the abundance of the heart, the mouth speaks." - Luke 6:45b.

"God who gives life to the dead and calls those things which do not exist as though they do." - Romans 4:17b

13.2. Fervent prayer examples aimed at offering comfort and resilience. Please customize this prayer. "Dear heavenly Father, I thank you first for sustaining me along this grueling path as I seek to do your will for _____. I come to you today in need of Your help, I am close to despair, please give me the courage, the strength, and the stamina to go forward with my tasks at hand. This is a difficult stage, and I need Your wisdom to know when to let go of the reins and to get more help. I am exhausted, mentally, physically, and emotionally. I daily trust You and wait on Your answers. Do what You do best, send me peace and practical wisdom to care for _____ well. As I rely on You, let me know and see Your power, Your love and Your answers. In Jesus name, Amen." He will answer you, and your faith will be strengthened because you came to Him in humility and faith.

"God resists the proud but gives grace to the humble." - James 4:6

"No, in all these things we are more than conquerors through him who loved us. For I am sure that neither death nor life, nor angels nor rulers, nor things present nor things to come, nor powers, nor height nor depth, nor anything else in all creation, will be able to separate us from the love of God in Christ Jesus our Lord." - Romans 8: 37-39

"You are of God (little children) and have overcome them because greater is He who is in you than he who is in the world." - I John 4:4

13.3. Pray and meditate in the daily caregiving routine. Begin the day in prayers of gratitude and hope, "Seek first the kingdom of

God…" and end the day with "Come to me, all you who are weary and burdened, and I will give you rest." At frustrating times when you're at your weakest, if all you can muster at the moment is, "Lord help me", by all means, pray that. He hears, cares, and will give you both what you need. I have found it is not usually in the form I expected or the way I envisioned but He does come through. Keep thanking Him till then. We cannot order God to do exactly as we want, like a customer in a restaurant. We make specific unselfish requests in faith and let Him provide His answers in His way and in His timing. We do not know the comprehensive future, and as human beings, we tend to catastrophize what we don't know. Or we tend to minimize it and are in denial of the hard truth. Either way, God knows, and He will arrange the best for you both.

"For My thoughts are not your thoughts, nor are your ways My ways," says the Lord. "For as the heavens are higher than the earth, so are My ways higher than your ways, and My thoughts than your thoughts." - Isaiah 55:8-9.

"In the same way, the Spirit helps in our weaknesses. For we do not know what we should pray for as we ought, but the Spirit Himself makes intercession for us with wordless groans. And He who searches our hearts knows the mind of the Spirit, because the Spirit intercedes for God's people in accordance with the will of God." - Romans 8:26-27.

*"Finally, brethren, whatever things are true, whatever things are noble, whatever things are just, whatever things are pure, whatever things are lovely, whatever things are of good report, if there is any virtue and if there is anything praiseworthy—**meditate** on these things." -* Philippians 4:8

13.4. When praying about the unfairness of dementia, it is tempting to ask, "Why God?" and get angry when we don't see an answer. It is OK to be angry at God for a season, just do not stay there as it may turn into bitterness. Bitterness is devil's food, one of his devious delights. We do not know the exact answer to why, but we do know this: "We live our lives in the eye of God, and not at the periphery, but at the center of His vision, His concern." (Peck, 1978, p. 311) The sovereign Lord is aware of our situation and will bring good out of it if we surrender to His will that is found in scripture. Feed yourself Biblical truths to find comfort and courage to persevere in peace. When you are finally able to, pray and ask Him, "What God?" "What do You want of me?" "What can I do or say to bring a bit more clarity, and some comfort and peace for both of us?" Recognizing those times when it's **you** that needs His help most, because the constant tasks at hand are too much for mere mortals, a true Higher Power is necessary to make some sense of this intrusive disorder and help to not just understand the eternal impact of caregiving, but to make these difficult days your life's finest hours. That may sound wildly strange, but it is just the kind of work the Lord does. Throughout time, God has been known to permit something He hates to achieve something He loves. The most perfect example is His brutal, vivid death at the hands of humans. Then His marvelous resurrection at the hands of God! Another example is in Genesis, where Joseph is talking to his brothers about the devious deed they did to him.

"But as for you, you meant evil against me; but God meant it for good." - Genesis 20:50

13.5. Have you ever heard it said, "Why on earth God, would You let this happen?" That question is common and can be observed in the presence of inexplicable, deadly natural disasters like tornados, or earthquakes, etc. Then there are deliberate human natural disasters when cruel and evil people harm or kill the innocent. Dementia is not just a human disaster, nor is it only a vast natural disaster, it is some of both. The question to God, "why on earth," is the key. Heaven is His domain, not that He has no power on earth,

He certainly does. God exerts complete control, though due to original sin, God has temporarily put Satan on a leash over earth's domain. Satan is called the *prince of the power of the air* here. "...in which you once walked according to the course of this world, according to the prince of the power of the air, the spirit who now works in the sons of disobedience." Ephesians 2:2 Satan is the author of all the evil that goes on here.

Problems and catastrophes come to mankind often without cause, without permission, and without obvious reasons. The Almighty is not on His throne in heaven, wringing His hands in confusion as to how this malady came to be. He has an eternal, divine purpose for it. All people on earth suffer in some way, Christians included. The human condition is lived out in a hostile, sin-filled world. We live on a battleground, not a playground. (The Invisible War, Ingram, 2015, p.61) Yet that doesn't mean we are always in a battle, though we are not to be ignorant of the schemes of the opposition. The questions concerning disasters and tragedies have challenged sages and scholars alike. With this truth rising to the top, God is good and in charge, and we can trust him, come-what-may. We must be persuaded that *"we do not fight for victory, but from victory."* (Ingram, 2015, p.68) It is a query that we must accept that there are no specific answers here on earth, but plenty of answers in heaven. In this life, it is all a test. Being a dementia caregiver may be more about you, storing up rewards in heaven, than having a comfortable life.

"For we must all appear before the judgment seat of Christ, so that each one may be paid back according to what he has done while in the body, whether good or evil." - II Corinthians 5:10

"Strengthening the souls of the disciples, exhorting them to continue in the faith, and saying, "We must, through many tribulations enter the kingdom of God." - Acts 14:22.

13.6. A dementia caregiver has been assigned to a tough job by showing patient love and care to the 'least of these'. If you still ask why, it is important to understand that one reason a person may acquire dementia is for the caregiver to learn, experience, and share how to love those with the disorder. Your DP may have it for God's glory and for the comfort of others who are beginning their trek down the same path. As Pastor Rick Warren said, the Christian life is not about us, it is to bring pleasure to God. (Warren, 2002) "Obviously, I'm not trying to win the approval of people, but of God. If pleasing people were my goal, I would not be Christ's servant." Galatians 1:10 NLT

The second purpose of our lives is to love fellow members of God's family unselfishly. Clearly, dementia fits the bill for these two altruistic goals. God is far more interested in growing our character than our comfort. Loving someone who is hard to love is also what Jesus modeled so well. It is a lifelong path to love in the face of criticism, even contempt. As M. Scot Peck wrote, "Love is the will to extend one's self for the purpose of nurturing one's own or another's spiritual growth. Love is as love does. Love is an act of will—namely, both an intention and an action. Will also implies choice. We do not have to love. We choose to love." (Peck, 2003)

"We love because He loved us first." - I John 4:19

"Love is patient, love is kind, it is not envious. Love does not brag, it is not puffed up. It is not rude, it is not self-serving, it is not easily angered or resentful. It is not glad about injustice but rejoices in the truth. It bears all things, believes all things, hopes all things, endures all things. Love never fails." - I Corinthians 13:4-8a.

14

HARNESSING FAITH IN TIMES OF CHALLENGE: WAYS TO GAIN EMOTIONAL RESILIENCE

S trategies for overcoming moments of doubt and maintaining faith. Doubt creeps in stealthily, a whisper that questions one's capacity, the purpose behind the pain, and the presence of divine support. In these moments, the scriptures offer a bulwark against despair. James 1:2-5 and Romans 8:28 remind caregivers that trials are not void of purpose; they are opportunities for growth, for deepening faith, and for witnessing the unfolding of divine plans. The reflection on these verses becomes an exercise in refocusing, shifting from the immediacy of daily struggles to the broader, higher goals of spiritual growth and divine orchestration. Since God is the manager, the author, and the finisher of our faith, everything happens for a reason. We are all more than the sum total of life's experiences. Even the bad and challenging has a cumulative positive value.

It is in this stage of our lives that we need to refuse to indulge in self-pity as it is a deep rut of despair that is harder to get out of than to avoid. Tell yourself the truth; life on earth has problems, and no one is spared of them. Mine and my DP's problems are just for a season. But they will add value to our lives in eternity if our care philosophy mirrors scripture the majority of the time (no one is perfect). When looking at all the horrors in our world today, Pastor Dan Plourde says, "It's not falling apart; it's falling into place." The musical group Casting Crowns uses a similar term in a wonderful song, *Just Be Held.* This means that the prophetic words in scripture are coming to pass in our generation. We must be Kingdom-minded rather than carnally-minded. Please read the following verses carefully and meditate on them.

*"My brethren, **count** it all joy when you fall into various trials, knowing that the testing of your faith produces patience. But let patience have its perfect work, that you may be perfect and complete, lacking nothing. If any of you lacks wisdom, let him ask of God, who gives to all liberally and without reproach, and it will be given to him." -* James 1: 2-5.

"God blesses those who patiently endure testing and temptation. Afterward, they will receive the crown of life that God has promised to those who love Him." - James 1:12. NLT.

"All things work together for good to those who love the Lord and are called according to His purposes." - Romans 8:28.

14.2. The importance of seeking professional help when stress becomes overwhelming, including counseling and therapy options. Often caregivers themselves may have behavioral health issues that need to be addressed. If they are not addressed, the caregivers themselves may become depressed or filled with anxiety. Sometimes medication may help. Seeing a therapist does not indicate an absence or even a weakening of your faith, it shows you are a smart, alert human being. Recognizing the signs that additional help is needed, whether in the form of counseling, therapy, or medical intervention, is a crucial aspect of effective caregiving. It is important to differentiate between clinical depression and fleeting moments of honest sadness and disappointment. This acknowledgment is not a concession of defeat but an affirmation of the caregiver's commitment to providing the best possible care, a recognition that strength is found in the wisdom to seek assistance. The counsel of professionals, whether garnered through a social worker, direct consultation or the resources provided by support organizations, offers caregivers an accurate picture and a way forward in hope with new tools in their toolbelt.

A good therapist or counselor can help you navigate the complex emotions you are feeling as well as help make sense of some new emotions that have arisen as you've taken on the significant role of caregiver. These professionals can help you see any blind spots and show you how to become aware of any *triggers* that cause friction or worse. A trigger typically refers to something that instantly prompts a strong emotional response or reaction in a person. These triggers can vary widely and may be related to past experiences, trauma, or deeply ingrained beliefs (even false beliefs). They can be powerful and deeply personal saboteurs affecting one in profound ways and influencing our thoughts, emotions, and behaviors. Triggers are easy to see in other people, it's often evidenced by "flying off the handle" or overreacting to an otherwise harmless thing or words. It can be due to Post Traumatic Stress Disorder, which again is easier to spot in others. PTSD is not always associated with military combat; it is a byproduct of any unhealed trauma. Often reacting to a trigger is a negative experience fraught with outbursts, rage, and/or aggressive urges toward violence. It can also initiate other reactions, like crying, running away, and highly fearful behaviors. These episodes are from obsolete yet unfinished business that still inhabits the adult person. The emotional brain keeps generating heightened sensations about something that happened long ago. (Van Der Kolk, 2014, p. 210)

Being a dementia caregiver, especially in the latter stages, has many possible scenarios where one might be triggered. Becoming self-aware is the beginning of healing, it is at the core of recovering from those unbearable sensations. (Van Der Kolk 2014, p. 210) The point is not to avoid them but to feel them fully in the presence of a safe and wise counselor because unfortunately "unresolved trauma can take a terrible toll on relationships." (Van Der Kolk, 2014, p. 213) It is important to deal with these as soon as you can for your emotional well-being and that of your family.

If you are a fortunate one whose triggers no longer overpower you, then understanding this can help you to be compassionate for those who still deal with them.

"God is our refuge and strength a very present help in trouble. Therefore, we will not fear even though the earth be removed and though the mountains carried into the midst of the sea." - Psalm 46:1-2.

14.3. Your DP, too, may have their own triggers of unfinished business, but at this point in their life, it must remain unfinished here on earth. Only God can heal their soul as their mind has enough to deal with. A person with dementia or specifically Alzheimer's, has changed so much over time that being irritable or aggressive is most likely not caused by any past trauma that triggers them; it is caused by the disease itself. With or without emotional triggers, a good counselor is well worth the time and money (if necessary) to improve your personal caregiving quality of life along with its longevity and effectiveness. Remember that a good counselor will recommend how to make your life better, they cannot change your DP. But by giving you choices to change certain aspects of yourself, it can certainly influence anyone around you, including your DP.

"Where there is no counsel, the people fall: but in the multitude of counselors there is safety." - Proverbs 11:14

"For by wise counsel you will wage your own war, and in a multitude of counselors there is victory." - Proverbs 24:6.

14.4. Biblical meditation is focusing on and repeating to oneself the truth of God's promises. It can be coupled with prayers of release and trust so that we no longer carry our heavy burdens. Mindfulness is a deliberate repositioning to notice what, who, how, and where we are. It is also about focus, to take us out of the automatic state of doing something rote. We are present and alert to our context. We have self-awareness as well as others' awareness. The dual practices of meditation and mindfulness bring caregivers back to the present, anchoring you amidst the tempest of emotions and responsibilities. Through these practices, focusing on the promises of God while engaging in mindful breathing, caregivers can find a center of calm. This center acts as a pivot, a point from which all actions and decisions emanate, grounded in peace and clarity. As outlined in Galatians 5:22-23, the fruit of the Spirit becomes qualities that caregivers can draw on from within, transforming their inner landscape into one of love, joy, peace, and self-control. It is far easier to get our tanks emotionally and spiritually filled before our time with the DP so that we are not stressed to the breaking point. Meditating on God's promises and being mindful of so much good that happens around us are two keys to staying emotionally sober. If you are in pain, emotional or physical, it certainly will burst out in unpleasant and unexpected ways. C.S. Lewis speaks to this point well; "...Pain insists upon being attended to. God whispers to us in our pleasures, speaks in our conscience, but shouts in our pains: it is His megaphone to rouse a deaf world." (Lewis, 1948, p. 81) Most of the time, the Lord speaks to us in a still, small voice. It is a wise person who listens to and responds to His leanings.

"And behold, the Lord passed by, and a great and strong wind tore into the mountains and broke the rocks in pieces before the Lord, but the Lord was not in the wind; and after the wind an earthquake, but the Lord was not in the earthquake; and after the earthquake a fire, but the Lord was not in the fire; and after the fire, a still small voice." - I Kings 19:11-12

14.5. Journaling can help process emotions and document the caregiving journey. A caregiver's journal offers a dual benefit: it serves as an emotional outlet and a tangible record of their journey. This practice allows for the processing of complex emotions, the celebration of small victories, and the chronicling of the caregiving experience. The words you write down will be a wonderful personal diary of the last years, months, and days of your DP's life, as well as your amazing work. This diary will become a most treasured possession and a testimony of your dedication and of God's faithfulness. Some people have a loved one die in a fiery auto crash, with a sudden catastrophic accident, in a fatal heart attack or stroke, or with painful cancer. One good thing to consider is that with dementia, or Alzheimer's specifically, the person doesn't die instantly; it is, on average, 5 to 10 years later. I suggest that, if at all possible, you document these days, even if it's mostly monotonous or there's not much to write about. For that kind of week, try to think of one interesting thing to say. Another week may be full of things to say. Along with the mundane, there will be some stories that will be scary, quite funny, touching, and even happy. The rest of the family will certainly be grateful for this record of both yours and the DP's legacy. They can either add to it or write their own.

"Moses wrote down their starting places, stage by stage, by command of the Lord, and these are their stages according to their starting places." - Numbers 33:2

"The days of our lives are seventy years, and if by reason of strength they are eighty years, yet their boast is only labor and sorrow; for it is soon cut off, and we fly away." "So teach us to number our days, that we may gain a heart of wisdom." - Psalm 90: 10 & 12.

14.6. The role of practicing gratitude is to maintain a positive outlook. It is critical to cultivate a practice of gratitude, even in the midst of challenging caregiving situations, because it has such a strong positive impact on your emotional well-being. In the daily grind practicing gratitude can significantly alter one's perspective. Recognizing and cherishing moments of connection, beauty, and grace amidst the challenges can shift the focus from what is lost to what remains. Gratitude highlights the divine presence and provision in even the smallest details. It is also a barometer of your emotional tank. If it feels fake or impossible to find something to be grateful for, it generally means you're in dire need of a break and respite care for the DP. A trip to the beach, a lake, or your favorite sight is called for, weather permitting. Maybe it's time to take in a comedy at the theater or a long walk in the park. Whatever way you positively refresh your focus, do this.

Stay away from comparing your situation with any others. Focus on what there is to be grateful for, not what is lacking. A grateful heart attracts blessings, as a complaining or jealous heart attracts misery. On the other hand, comparing your situation to others is dangerous, as envy can eat us alive, so to speak. When tempted to sink into sadness, proclaim and sing the old Don Moen song, "Give Thanks."

> *"Give thanks with a grateful heart (with a grateful heart). Give thanks to the Holy One (to the Holy One). Give thanks because He's given Jesus Christ, His Son. And now let the weak say, I am strong. Let the poor say, I am rich because of what the Lord has done for us. Give thanks. We give thanks to You."*

"A tranquil spirit revives the body, but envy is rottenness to the bones." - Proverbs 14:30

"Forty years You sustained them in the wilderness; They lacked nothing; Their clothes did not wear out and their feet did not swell." - Nehemiah 9:21

"Rejoice always, pray without ceasing, in everything give thanks; for this is the will of God in Christ Jesus for you." - I Thessalonians 5:16-18

14.7. The caregiver's connection with nature can have the same spiritual and emotional healing benefits as the DP. Stepping into nature offers a profound source of rejuvenation and spiritual connection. The scriptures speak of the divine hand in the creation of the earth, the seas, and all living things, reminding caregivers of the beauty and majesty that surrounds you. Nature serves as a tangible expression of divine creativity and care, a space where the soul can find rest and the mind can regain perspective. The mountains or ocean can be a tangible visual of God's enormity and power. But, if all you have is a porch, it is still possible to add a bit of natural color and texture to focus on and lift your spirit. Everywhere there is a sky; lookup on clear days to see the beauty and feel fresh hope. If you live in a crowded city or an apartment, there are still sanctuaries of nature to be sought at a park or as you pass by your neighbors who have the time and skills to make their yards beautiful. If you imagine they beautified it just for you, it can encourage gratitude and joy. Engaging in simple outdoor activities or just sitting in a garden can become a spiritual practice, a time of communion with the Creator, and a momentary respite from the demands of caregiving.

"In his hand are the depths of the earth; the heights of the mountains are his also. The sea is his, for he made it, and his hands formed the dry land." - Psalm 95:4-5

"And out of the ground the Lord God made to spring up every tree that is pleasant to the sight and good for food. - Genesis 2:9

"Let the heavens rejoice, let the earth be glad; let the sea resound, and all that is in it. Let the fields be jubilant, and everything in them; let all the trees of the forest sing for joy." - Psalm 96:11-12

15

HOME SAFE TECHNOLOGY

Home safety technologies can assist in caring for a loved one with dementia, enhancing both safety and independence. In the quest to create a sanctuary that both nurtures and protects, caregivers turn to an arsenal of home safety technologies designed with the unique challenges of dementia care in mind. Devices that once seemed born of futuristic fantasy now offer practical solutions to everyday concerns. Motion sensors discreetly monitor movement, illuminating paths to safeguard against the dangers of unseen obstacles in the night. Doors, cabinets, the kitchen stove, or the toaster oven are all potential harbors for hazards. They can be secured with a safety switch or smart locks, their status monitored via smartphone, ensuring that dangerous items remain off or inaccessible. Cameras become benign sentinels and offer caregivers the peace of mind that comes with visual assurance, whether it's to check in during a moment of silence or to observe sleep patterns. This integration of technology into the caregiving environment does more than mitigate risks; it fosters a sense of independence for the individual with dementia, offering them the desire for freedom within the bounds of safety.

"The eyes of the Lord are in every place, keeping watch on the evil and the good." - Proverbs 15:3

15.2. Pros and Cons of telehealth technology services for caregiver support and patient care, including convenience and access to specialists. The advent of telehealth marks a paradigm shift in the caregiver's toolkit, offering a bridge between the homebound individual and the broader medical community. This digital conduit, spanning the chasm that often isolates those in the throes of dementia from essential medical care, brings the expertise of specialists into the home. Consulting with a neurologist via video call can alleviate much anxiety, bypassing the logistical hurdles of transportation and the disorientation that often accompanies changes in environment for someone with dementia. Telehealth services extend beyond mere convenience, offering access to specialists who might otherwise be unreachable due to location constraints, ensuring that care is both comprehensive and tailored. For the caregiver, telehealth provides a means to participate actively in the medical dialogue, ask questions, seek clarifications, and advocate effectively for their loved one, all from the safety and comfort of the familiar.

The cons are that the video screen doctor may confuse your DP even more or that the Dr. doesn't necessarily witness the entire situation or their body language. Using your computer screen, this video appointment can be almost as good as going to the doctor in person, especially when the appointment is routine or a follow-up. When the DP simply cannot or will not leave the home, it is a valid option. Another pro is that you don't have to go through the effort to get your DP ready and out the door in time to make the appointment.

"Jesus answered and said to them, 'Those who are well have no need of a physician, but those who are sick.'" - Luke 5:31

15.3. The "nanny cam" video, which was originally invented to watch the baby in their crib, or the nanny themselves, while parents are out, is now a popular and helpful tool to monitor the DP while you're not in the room with them. These cameras are truly a positive technology to give you another set of eyes, so to speak, inside your home. **SimpliSafe** offers a variety of whole-house security packages. A **RING** or **WYZE** doorbell shows on your smartphone who is outside your home whether you're there or not. These are about $120-$250 (retail price) plus a small monthly service fee to maintain the video feed. No private passwords or pins are required. They are hardwired to your original doorbell or fastened with an adhesive if there is no doorbell.

Amidst the embrace of digital tools, the shadow of privacy concerns looms, a reminder of the vulnerability inherent in the sharing and storing of personal information. Caregivers treat these intimate details entrusted to their care with caution. Encryption becomes the watchword, its presence a barrier against unwelcome eyes. Passwords, those digital keys to personal realms, are crafted with complexity, their combination a shield protecting against intrusion. The selection of apps and gadgets, therefore, is not merely a matter of functionality but of security, ensuring that the benefits of technology are not marred by risks to privacy. This vigilant approach to digital security underscores the sacred trust between caregiver and care recipient. It is critically important to backup all passwords, ID numbers, and any personal information on a hardcopy book that is kept under a tangible lock and key. These are *never* to be kept anywhere online, in your email folders, or in the cloud. Far too many sites have been hacked, so it is best to keep the hardcopy in a fireproof and water-resistant natural domain.

"The Lord preserves those with knowledge, but he ruins the plans of the treacherous." - Proverbs 22:12

15.4. Scams that come via technology, from cellphone/landline, or regular postal mail, etc. Amid the digital age's marvels, a shadow looms, cast by those who would exploit the vulnerabilities of declining conditions and advancing age. Caregivers, vigilant sentinels, must thus extend their watch to the realm of communication, guarding against the insidious threat of scams that target the elderly and those with dementia. The cunning of these deceitful schemes knows no bounds, from robocalls that mimic the urgency of legitimate concerns to phishing emails draped in the guise of official correspondence. The caregiver's role evolves to include educator and shield, imparting wisdom on the dangers of unsolicited calls and emails and instilling a practice of caution and verification. Strategies to fortify defenses include the simple yet effective measure of screening calls, the use of call-blocking technologies, and the meticulous oversight of mail, both digital and physical. In imparting these practices, caregivers not only protect their loved ones from the tangible losses that scams can inflict but also shield their peace of mind, preserving the sanctity of their sanctuary against the intrusion of predatory deceit.

These should be a high priority to assertively look for. This is an important warning for anyone, regardless of mental acuity or age. Yet for someone with dementia, they are especially vulnerable to the schemes, tricks, and devious strategies of these cruel predators. There are endless ways the thieves try to get your and your loved one's money, property, and peace of mind. Even your or their very identity can be stolen. There are also several ways to prevent these attempts from reaching your DP, but they all are related to you needing to be a doorkeeper to their electronic devices, phones, emails, etc. Predators deliberately prey on older people for the very reason that many are less likely to notice the red flags that others may see. It is better, by far, to accidentally insult a stranger than lose their life's savings or any savings. Every time I answer an unknown phone number, I always say, "Who's calling, please?" in a kind voice. Never do I automatically say "hello" if I don't know the caller. That's because if it's a robocall, it is dialed by a computer that's programmed to start talking when hearing the word *hello*. If it is then silent on the other end of the call, it indicates that it is either a solicitor or a scammer.

"A prudent person foresees danger and takes precautions. The simpleton goes blindly on and suffers the consequences." - Proverbs 22:3

15.5. When to withdraw certain technologies. If your DP still possesses a cell phone, landline phone, personal computer (PC) or Apple Mackintosh computer (MAC), tablet, etc. it may be time to allow these to be used only under close supervision. Even USPS (snail mail) still has scams to watch out for, though most occur online or on a cell phone. Publishers Clearing House still exists to sell cheap garbage to naïve people, thinking it will help them win big money. Your DP may order excessive items without realizing they are spending real money. Most online stores or ads make it so easy to buy. Your DP may not know that Amazon will not call them asking for credit card information or that their bank will not call to warn them about 'someone trying to withdraw funds, and all they have to do is to confirm their account numbers' or that a text from the (fake) USPS will not send a message saying a 'parcel is awaiting their complete address to deliver it' when all this thief wants is for them to tap the text link and pick up malware that can really make a mess and steal whatever is available to steal. They may not know about the dangers of home title fraud or social security fraud. The schemes are as rampant, crafty, and dangerous as flu viruses, and there are new tricks daily. Beware, be skeptical, and be warned. This may be done respectfully, but not at the cost of painful losses. The truth about our world is that it's filled with darkness and deception. It is still better to be safe than sorry.

"And Jesus answered and said to them: "Take heed that no one deceives you." - Matthew 24:4

"Look, I am sending you out as sheep among wolves. So be as shrewd as snakes and harmless as doves." - Matthew 10:16

16

STRESS MANAGEMENT SOLUTIONS AND STRATEGIES FOR MAINTAINING SERENITY

The signs of stress in caregivers often mirror the quiet creep of dusk—gradual yet unmistakable once acknowledged. It manifests in sleepless nights spent replaying the day's challenges, in the tightening of shoulders as the next task approaches, and the shortness of breath accompanying moments of overwhelm. For caregivers, the crucial first step lies in discerning these signals amidst the cacophony of daily responsibilities. Acknowledging stress is akin to spotting the first signs of wear in a well-used garment; early detection allows for timely mending, preventing the fabric from unraveling further.

Mastering the flow of time, with its relentless demands and finite supply, stands at the heart of stress reduction. Effective time management for caregivers transcends the mere allocation of tasks; it involves the discernment to prioritize, the wisdom to delegate, and the courage to set aside time for self-renewal. Strategies such as the Eisenhower Box, originally called the Eisenhower Matrix, is a time management tool that helps prioritize tasks based on their urgency and importance, it's the idea of a medical triage unit. It is named after Dwight D. Eisenhower, the 34th President of the United States, who famously said, "What is important is seldom urgent and what is urgent is seldom important." This matrix can transform an overwhelming list into a manageable plan of action. The technique of time-blocking reserves spaces within the day for focused care activities, personal rest, and those unplanned moments that inevitably arise. This is not a literal box; it is a large whiteboard hung on the wall with dry-erase markers to fill in the day's priority in segments. Delineate four large rectangles, each with a prioritized list of the day's duties. I would separate them by time. They were originally labeled with: Do, Decide, Delegate, Delete, sections. But you can customize it to what works for you.

The whiteboard may look like this:

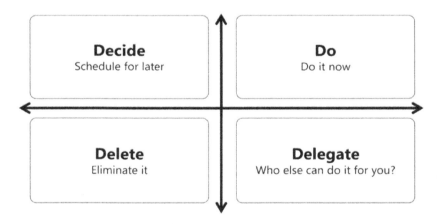

Remind yourself that these days here on earth do not have the final say, God does, and heaven holds the eternal rewards for your actionable love and sincere devotion. As M. Scot Peck wrote, "The journey of spiritual growth is a path of lifelong learning. You never arrive at a place where you have learned everything you need to know. The effort to grow and learn must continue until the day you die."

"Therefore, as the elect of God, holy and beloved, put on tender mercies, kindness, humility, meekness, longsuffering; bearing with one another, and forgiving one another, if anyone has a complaint against another; even as Christ forgave you, so you also must do." - Colossians 3:11-13

16.2. Healthy stress busters: Simple yet effective strategies abound to alleviate stress. Physical activity, from a brisk walk in the freshness of the morning to the deliberate movements of chair exercises or stretches, serves as a powerful stress reliever, channeling tension into motion and clarity. Creative expression, whether through painting, writing, or crafting, offers a release, a way to channel emotions into tangible forms. The creation of a Memory Box is one way. This is described in the next section.

Even the act of laughter shared over a cup of tea with a friend or through the pages of a light-hearted book or a joke magazine can lift the weight of stress, reminding caregivers of the joy that persists amidst the trials.

Be aware of ways to deal with stress that can backfire on you. In the shadow of stress, pitfalls await—temporary solaces that promise relief but deliver further strain. The lure of substance use, the seduction of endless hours lost to screen time, or the withdrawal toward isolation each offer a false sanctuary. Recognizing these temptations for what they are, traps that ensnare rather than liberate is crucial. The path forward lies not in escape but in engagement, in seeking solutions that nourish rather than deplete, that build resilience rather than erode it.

"God who comforts us in all our tribulation, that we may be able to comfort those who are in any trouble, with the comfort with which we ourselves are comforted by God." - II Corinthians 1:3-4.

16.3. Together you can create a literal *Memory Box* that may help to anchor the DP when they are frustrated, bored, or need a distraction at any time. It is best to start this box earlier when the DP can help choose what goes in it and help elaborate on the story behind each item. This is a cherished portable container, a compilation of many good mementos in the DP's life that bring comfort, laughter, and happy memories. This box acts as a key, unlocking doors to feelings that dementia has, over time, closed. It is not just for high anxiety moments but should be seen as a wonderful source of inspiration anytime.

It is a tangible box containing certain pieces of the essence of their life. This may extend to the vessel itself by personalization. Perhaps the box is adorned with a fabric reminiscent of a favored dress, constructed of wood from a cherished project, or has a collage of textures and pictures to represent the DP. The contents of a memory box, as diverse and unique as the individuals they represent, contain items that are selected as linear points of time in their life stories. Ideas to include are photographs of these; their wedding, of the first home or apartment, favorite car(s), or the children when they were young, or other significant milestones, etc. Also include personal mementos: postcards from a trip, old personal pins and honors, a graduation cap, maybe a handkerchief imbued with lots of memories, perhaps a well-worn baseball glove, a delicate piece of heirloom jewelry, a bottle of their favorite cologne, or a vinyl record of a favorite album. Any smaller-sized item that carries a bit of happy personal history of positive experiences and feelings. Artifacts from hobbies and passions, be it a paintbrush or a recipe card, a fishing lure that caught the big one, a girl/boy scout sash or cap, a job retirement watch, etc.,

Everyone can celebrate the individual's interests, inviting engagement that reinforces a sense of self by stimulating sensory memories. It is such a joy to see when bits of memory surface, if only for a moment.

Whether detailed on an accompanying card or shared orally, the narrative attached to each item enriches the experience, providing context that invites the individual to explore the item and the memories it represents. While they still can, it may be fun to record the DP talking about the item and its memory. Then replay it to them later, or just for yourself.

If this memory box becomes frustrating, it has lost its purpose, and it is time to relegate it to a safe place for the family to enjoy or give it another try on a better day. Once again, discernment is required to avoid it being thrown across the room in anger.

"I have come that they may have life and that they may have it more abundantly." - John 10"10b

"For all the promises of God in Him are Yes, and in Him, Amen." - II Corinthians 1:20

16.4 Pacing may be a concern or an irritation for you. If you deal with the DP's excessive pacing, it may take a few clever questions from you to investigate to possibly find the culprit. Once discovered, you may eliminate the issue and thus eliminate the pacing, hopefully. Dementia-induced pacing is common but, in itself, is not harmful. If it continues too long, it can lead to dizziness, which may lead to a fall. Of course, you can try giving your DP something else to do. Have them "dust" an area and show them how, or give them a simple, safe task and model it first. Or have them bring the garbage cans to you, if this was a former regular job and they still understand the meaning. I suggest you make it a habit to look in the cans before throwing the bag away. People with dementia have been known to put all kinds of good things, like keys, glasses, TV remote, someone's dental partial, jewelry, etc. in a garbage can.

As a rule, the trash cans are the first place to look when something is missing, then the refrigerator, toilet, etc.

Pacing can be a sign of possible underlying issues, indicating that the person may be experiencing some form of distress or unmet need. Consider these possibilities.

- **Anxiety or Stress.** Pacing can be a coping mechanism for anxiety, agitation, or stress. It may help the person feel more in control or provide a sense of purpose.
- **Boredom.** Individuals with dementia might pace if they are not sufficiently engaged or stimulated. Lack of activities can lead to restlessness and pacing.
- **Physical Discomfort.** Pacing can be a response to physical discomfort or pain that the DP cannot communicate verbally.
- **Need to Use the Bathroom.** Sometimes, it shows a need to use the bathroom, but the DP might not be able to recognize or communicate this need clearly.
- **Searching for Something or Someone.** The person may be looking for something familiar, such as a loved one, a place, or an object.
- **Medication Side Effects.** Some medications can cause restless pacing as a side effect. Your pharmacist is the best source to ask about drug interactions and side effects.
- **Sleep Disturbances.** Poor sleep patterns or disruptions in circadian rhythms can lead to increased activity and pacing during the day or night. (Alzheimer's Association) (Dementia Australia) (National Institute on Aging)

Your DP cannot always articulate what they feel, or they don't know the difference between a minor cold and something more serious. A headache is not visible, and neither are many ailments.

You might check every obvious symptom, such as a fever, a cut or splinter, coughing, or runny nose, and act accordingly. If you're really concerned, call the doctor and explain what you see if you've already done a decent investigation. A trip to the bathroom may or may not resolve it. If it is just boredom engaging them may stop the pacing for a while. Sincerely pray for discernment. Then, having done all, choose to accept this quirky habit rather than try to change it.

"Do not judge according to appearance, but judge with righteous judgment." - John 7:24

"Deal with Your servant according to Your mercy and teach me Your statutes. I am Your servant; give me understanding." - Psalm 119:124-125a.

17

PERSONAL STORIES

These are my real-life stories as a caregiver when I found practical wisdom and faith through experience. There are moments of tenderness and joy in caregiving as well as funny or dangerous moments.

Personal story #1. The filter is missing. I was to take her out for breakfast. I would ask her husband what she liked ahead of time so that I could order the food. I also did this to make sure it was nutritionally balanced and to keep her from being confused and appearing unable to read the menu. We usually sat in silence waiting for the drinks and meals to arrive. But this day she wanted to talk. She noticed other guests having their breakfast and she said things out loud about them that most of us would keep inside our own private thoughts. Her words were not a nice compliment. I was embarrassed for her until she continued to speak, it soon became apparent that she was not rational. It was not my job to correct or scold her or even openly apologize to the people to whom she directed her comments. However, as we ate, I casually apologized to them without my DP's awareness. They too noticed her cognitive impairment and were not angry. Be aware that blurting out thoughts; having the filter removed, can be one of those unpleasant side effects of the disease.

17.2 Story #2. On occasion, my DP would try to get away from me, she was more than a wanderer, she was a runner! I took her to the movies one day and while I swiped the credit card to pay, she quietly took off without me. The second I looked up to take her hand, she was gone! I panicked some at first, then ran outside, knowing that if she was in the parking lot near strangers, that could be a very bad outcome. I asked a few people by the door if they saw her come out. I described her as a pretty, blond lady who is fit and tan, (she was not a stereotypical image of the disease). After hearing several no's, I went back inside, jogged down the corridor, and soon found her at the door of the theater where the movie we were to watch was shown. I calmly led her to a seat and learned a good lesson that day. I had prayed to God to always watch out for her and to keep me vigilant in my task to care for her. She still **tried** to run away from me now and then, but now I was aware of it and was never caught off guard again. I was so grateful that this event did not turn out badly. I thanked God for always watching out for us. See Chapter 22 on wandering devices.

17.3 Story #3. Be always forgiving and choose to forget. After watching the 2016 version of Pete's Dragon at the theater, we left walking very close together because I knew she was prone to run away. We got near a lady loading her car trunk with full bags when my DP started loudly stating that I was a stranger and was not allowed to take her. She called me some pretty bad names, some of it was absurd so the lady soon realized that my DP wasn't in her right mind. I had to remain calm, not take offense, and not explain to the lady that she had Alzheimer's. I would never want to share a private diagnosis or sound insulting. Fortunately, my DP saw the car we rode in and took off in that direction as fast as she could, and she was indeed fast. I unlocked the door via remote, on the way. Once in the car nothing at all was said except, "How did you like the movie?" I thanked God for protecting her over and over. I learned to keep moving forward, never backward in anger or regret. I let it go emotionally, but didn't let her go, visually!

17.4. Story #4. Identity confusion. I remember my DP, was so different one morning. She looked at me like I was her long-lost best friend. She gave me an extended hug like she didn't want to let go. She treated me like a beloved family member and wasn't at all skeptical of me. I imagined her believing I was someone from her past that she loved. It was a nice and starkly different attitude than what I was accustomed to. To my pleasant surprise, this mood lasted the whole day. I knew better than to ask her questions at this point, but to simply enjoy a respite from her generally disliking me, though it was more likely that she was uncertain of me. Most of the time I could see her confusion as to who I was to her and why I was around so much.

In the latter stages of dementia, a spouse, parent, or sibling may not know who you are. This is a hard and heartbreaking thing to experience. Yet it is not on purpose, of course, and it cannot be remedied by explaining the facts over and over. You can gently tell them your relationship, but it may not stick for long, if at all. Even the shared memories in the latter stages won't bring them back, except for a fleeting moment, then not at all. Just allow it, don't try to fix it, keep loving them, and stay close to your faith. They may think of you as a friendly stranger rather than a beloved family member. Sometimes, this can work in your favor because there are no preconceived notions of former family dynamics to wrangle and get cooperation with.

"Weeping may endure for a night, but joy comes in the morning." - Psalm 30:5

18

THE IMPACT OF DEMENTIA ON INTIMACY AND THE MARRIAGE RELATIONSHIP

As dementia reshapes your relationship, the process of navigating intimacy and connection requires resolve, resilience, and, finally, relinquishment. This chapter leans into the intricacies of sustaining emotional and physical closeness as dementia progresses, recognizing the relationship will alter, though the need for connection remains immutable.

Though literal closeness may not be the problem, some DPs become exceptionally insecure and needy in the early and middle stages and want to follow you everywhere. This is due to them knowing something is not right. Initially, they are partially aware of the advancing memory loss. It is a fearful thing, so they may shadow the spouse, partner, or caregiver to the point of being a nuisance. See Chapter 1 for nonverbal clues. This requires great sensitivity and creativity to handle well. Your spouse may become **like** your child in some ways. It is best not to think of them as a child but as a fearful adult with genuine insecurities caused by an illness.

Your boundaries with them will be challenged, but the DP is unaware of their stepping on them. It is not a good idea to excessively push back unless they are smothering you and won't even let you go to the bathroom alone. Safe distractions may give you a few moments of peace. They need ample reassurance and your comforting words. Let them sit by the bathroom door and speak to them while you're in there.

"Those who are planted in the house of the Lord shall flourish in the courts of our God. They shall still bear fruit in old age; they shall be fresh and flourishing." - Psalm 92: 13-15

"He brought me to the banqueting house, and his banner over me was love." - Song of Solomon 2:4

18.2. Dementia people still have their feelings and they are often not diminished; it is their knowledge and memories that are waning. They may indeed feel love for you and from you; yet they don't recall entirely what to do with it or how to show it. Nurturing intimacy and connection amidst dementia is an act of courage and creativity, honoring the present reality while cherishing the shared past. It is a journey where the essence of the relationship, transformed by the experience, reveals new depths of connection and resilience. The recalibration of expectations around the lack of, or the surplus of libido is not just necessary; it is evidence of the depth of your commitment and flexibility.

There will come a day, maybe you're there now, where this kind of intimacy is no longer viable. If this is still a small part of your life, physical intimacy often serves as both a conduit of love and a manifestation of connection. However, as dementia weaves its complex web, facets of the physical inevitably evolve and often disappear altogether. Being self-aware can lessen the impact by knowing when this area is off-limits and how to handle this loss. A selfless sensitivity to these changes becomes paramount. There are moments, or for the duration, when the person with dementia may no longer recognize their spouse, where the spark of desire dims, leaving a palpable void. In these times, the essence of love transcends physical expression, finding its voice in the quiet presence, the gentle touch that does not seek to invite passion but to convey harmony and comfort. Consider a moment or gesture of connection with your spouse that felt particularly meaningful. Reflect on the emotions it evoked and how it might inform new ways to express affection and maintain intimacy. The shift in behavior, the loss of words, demands that caregivers listen with more than their ears; they must tune into the emotional undercurrents, the unspoken needs. You may need to grieve over the loss and deal with it appropriately; maybe talk to a therapist. Once again, do not take their rejection personally; it is dementia's relentless forward motion at fault.

Caregivers' support in managing emotional needs outside of caregiving is not a luxury; it is a necessity. Whether composed of family, friends, or fellow travelers on the caregiving path, this support network serves as a lifeline. It is a reminder that while the caregiver's role is singular, you are not isolated in your experience. In practical terms, this might manifest in a weekly coffee with a friend who understands the unspoken weight of caregiving, offering a moment of reprieve and connection. This verse paints a vivid picture of this community of care, where mutual support and empathy underpin every interaction, reinforcing the caregiver's resilience and capacity to give.

"Be devoted to one another in love. Honor one another above yourselves. Never be lacking in zeal, but keep your spiritual fervor, serving the Lord. Be joyful in hope, patient in affliction, faithful in prayer." - Romans 12:10-15

18.3. The DP's response to your touch or kiss may be met with disdain or harsh rejection. It is critical to remember, once again, that this is dementia talking and doing, and do not take it personally. Their brain has scrambled messages which results in inappropriate and thus painful responses. For your sake, it is best to let your DP initiate the affection unless they are still in the early stages. In later stages, they may not know who you are, and to them, a kiss or hug is inappropriate and/or scary. Explore ways to maintain marital connection, focus on emotional and physical closeness rather than sexual. What this looks like varies. It may be wise to accept that this physical/intimate part of your life is over, but love remains *until death do us part.* Yet you still seek the good of your DP indefinitely, focusing on the sweet and fleeting moments that remain. This does not mean it is time to find a new spouse or a paramour. It is about self-sacrifice for this last season.

"I am my beloved's, and my beloved is mine." - Song of Solomon 6:3

> *"Through the windowpane she sees, a world that she no longer knows.*
> *Yet in her heart, a love remains, as strong as when it first arose.*
> *Though memories may fade away, and words become so hard to find,*
> *the love we shared will always stay, a beacon in her foggy mind."*
>
> - By John Bayley

18.4. Adjusting expectations around intimacy and relationships and finding new ways to express love and affection is essential. The issue of abandonment from your spouse with dementia may arise. Not that your spouse has intentionally done so, but it may feel like it. You are still married in a practical sense, but in so many ways, you live alone. This excerpt from The Davos Alzheimer's Collaborative, is especially profound. I hope it gives you some much-needed grace in times of emotional fatigue.

In Cathy's (the caregiver) case, Frank not only stopped expressing nuance and self-doubt, he also lost his ability to see his wife as a complete person. Cathy had become a prop, a vessel into whom he could pour all of his fixations, and so she found herself living with a humorless stranger with whom she had nothing in common. It's one of the heartbreaks of this disease. When someone we love develops cancer, patient and caregiver can commiserate, acknowledging the miseries of the disease while together experiencing, to some degree, a shared reality. But dementia at some point precludes this possibility. This strikes us as profoundly unfair because the collective reality that we once shared (and had come to expect) is now gone. Caregivers like Cathy experience such symptoms as relentless reminders that the emotional reciprocity that had once existed between her and Frank had disappeared—and there is nothing remotely fair about that. And though we may understand this unfairness intellectually, we are biologically disinclined to accept this. If, like Cathy, we're technically not alone but still feel alone, self-regulation becomes effortful, requiring mental energy that isn't always available. No wonder that after a long day of submitting to existential and mundane forms of unfairness, caregivers can become as volatile as the people they care for. (davosalzheimerscollaborative.org)

Over the years, dementia in a spouse can have multiple detrimental effects on you, not just them. As has been reiterated already, taking time away for yourself may save your life and your well-being. In this realization, you keep on caring for yourself as your DP would most certainly want for you, though it will undoubtedly be different. This verse is also for the care team, the body of Christ, and your friends & family who come along to help you and see that you get a refreshing time away from the demands of the DP.

"Even so, every good tree bears good fruit, but a bad tree bears bad fruit. Therefore, by their fruits you will know them." - Matthew 7: 17&20

"Give, and it will be given to you: good measure, pressed down, shaken together, and running over will be put into your bosom. For with the same measure that you use, it will be measured back to you." - Luke 6:38

UNDERSTANDING AND MANAGING SUNDOWNING: TIPS FOR THE LATE-DAY CHALLENGES

Within the complexities of dementia is a perplexing phenomenon known as sundowning, casting a shadow over the late hours of the day. However, the behavior is not exclusively in the evening. This condition, characterized by increased confusion, agitation, and restlessness (most often) as daylight wanes, poses a unique set of challenges for both the individual experiencing it and their caregivers. Symptoms extend beyond mere disorientation, manifesting in a spectrum of behaviors that range from mild irritability to intense anxiety or even hallucinations, transforming the twilight hours into a period of heightened attention and self-protective strategies for those providing care.

The medical reasons for sundowning remain shrouded in a veil of mystery, with theories suggesting a disruption in the circadian rhythms, an exacerbation of symptoms due to end-of-day exhaustion, hunger, fatigue, lack of sunshine, or the fierce frustration of not being able to talk like they once did. Regardless of its root cause, the effect on those ensnared by dementia's grip is palpable, with the fading light seemingly eroding the fragile hold they maintain over their environment and sense of self. For caregivers, this escalation of symptoms necessitates an approach that is both adaptive and compassionate, ensuring safety while striving to mitigate the distress experienced by your DP.

Sundowning not only amplifies the care demands placed upon caregivers but also serves as a stark reminder of dementia's pervasive reach, extending its influence into the rhythm and structure of daily life. The fluctuating intensity of the condition underscores the need for adjustments. It may be wise to get ahead of this phenomenon and ask for help during this day's segment. Make sure your smoke detector batteries are full, as accidents, like a kitchen fire, could result while you're trying to prepare dinner. To give more focus on the DP, instead of cooking at this time, many caregivers make the larger cooked meal at lunchtime or around 2 pm. In the evening, you may choose to microwave precooked meals (as mentioned in Chapter 9), order out, or have a soup that is easy to reheat. It is impossible to multitask well, so you'll need to make some adjustments during this time if your DP shows sundowning behavior.

"For He shall give His angels charge over you, to keep you in all your ways. In their hands, they shall bear you up, lest you dash your foot against a stone." - Psalm 91: 11-12

"He who dwells in the secret place of the Most High shall abide under the shadow of the Almighty. I will say of the Lord, "He is my refuge and my fortress My God, in Him I will trust." - Psalm 91:1

19.2. In confronting sundowning, caregivers must employ techniques that soothe and stabilize your DP. This might involve giving them a small healthy snack or drink, introducing soothing music to calm frayed nerves (yours and theirs), and dimming lights to reduce sensory overload. It could be helpful to steer them to sit and listen to music or a blog on a subject they used to like before dementia or watch a colorful show or cartoon for 30 minutes while you're preoccupied in the kitchen. I've found that speaking into your TV remote (or linking the TV to your YouTube channel) to find these kinds of videos: a fireplace fire, a babbling brook, the ocean's waves, star-filled galaxies, or horses running, etc., can help soothe and calm anyone through sights and sounds. Each action, though seemingly small, may help. Since their attention span is short, a cycle of different distractions could keep them entertained for a while. But there also may be days when nothing helps and the frustration piles high on you. This is when you will really need that extra person to assist you and/or the DP. It is a time to be creative and compassionate, as the DP is even more fearful than you are and cannot explain why.

During the day make sure your DP is exposed to the day's natural sunlight, weather permitting. Natural sunlight exposure has been linked to the regulation of mood and the prevention of mood disorders such as seasonal affective disorder, SAD. Sunshine stimulates the production of serotonin, a neurotransmitter associated with feelings of well-being and happiness. The sun also makes Vitamin D, which studies suggest may play a role in cognitive function and even the prevention of neurodegenerative diseases. Sufficient vitamin D levels may help maintain brain health and reduce the risk of cognitive decline. Absorption through the sun is more effective than a pill. This book will not elaborate on preventative measures, which is for another book entirely. See Chapter 30 for resources.

"Oh, how sweet the light of day, and how wonderful to live in the sunshine! Even if you live a long time, don't take a single day for granted." - Ecclesiastes 11:7-8. MSG.

19.3. The impact of sundowning can extend past the evening, influencing sleep patterns and, thus, the quality of life for both the

DP and caregiver. The disruption to nighttime rest can exacerbate the symptoms of dementia, creating a vicious cycle of fatigue and confusion that challenges the stamina and resourcefulness of even the most dedicated caregiver. When each person is sleep-deprived, it is critical to get help because mistakes are made when we are exhausted or weak. It is not a failure to recognize our humanity; again, it is strength to know when to fortify yourself.

A medical doctor may prescribe an anti-depressant or mood stabilizer, such as serotonin which is a chemical our bodies produce naturally. It's needed for the nerve cells and brain to function properly. These medications are called Selective Serotonin Reuptake Inhibitors (SSRI), they help stabilize one's mood and improve well-being. Though be aware of the possible side effects of insomnia. Please consult your physician about any medications that may interfere with sleep or exacerbate their symptoms. Your DP's doctor may have something else to prescribe without any sleep interference or direct you to natural solutions. As far as a pharmaceutical sedative to help the DP sleep and stay there, it should **not** be your first choice; it should be your last choice. There are numerous adverse side effects with sedatives that worsen memory and other dementia symptoms. Once again, seek professional advice here.

As mentioned in Chapter 10 on sleep, consider the natural sleep products that are listed there. These often lead to better sleep quality by encouraging deeper sleep. It also increases the amount of time that a user spends in REM, which is the period in which you will experience deep and truly restful sleep. Exposure to natural sunlight also helps regulate the body's internal clock and sleep-wake cycle, promoting better sleep quality and overall circadian rhythm regulation. See Chapter 9.

In this, the struggle against sundowning mirrors the broader battle against dementia itself—a contest not of strength but of perseverance, compassion, and a determined commitment to their well-being, come what may.

"To console those who mourn in Zion, to give them beauty for ashes, the oil of joy for mourning, the garment of praise for the spirit of heaviness; that they may be called trees of righteousness, the planting of the Lord, that He may be glorified." - Isaiah 61:3

19.4. Is sundowning inevitable or is it a possibility in the mid-dementia stage? The quick answer is no, it is not a universal symptom, but it appears in about 25% to 45% of patients. It is also not exclusive to dementia; it is a comorbid of other maladies as well. Navigating the complexities of sundowning requires a multifaceted strategy, one that encompasses environmental modifications, routine establishment, and, when necessary, the judicious use of medical interventions. The objective is not to erase the symptoms—often an impossible feat—but rather to create a buffer against the distress they cause, erecting an atmosphere of tranquility that counteracts any potential chaos that precedes the setting sun. This delicate balance, achieved through trial and error, shows the caregiver's peace-driven dedication.

"Do not ask me to remember, don't try to make me understand. Let me rest and know you're with me, kiss my cheek and hold my hand. I'm confused beyond your concept, I am sad and sick and lost. All I know is that I need you to be with me at all cost."

- by Owen Darnell

MAKE A DIFFERENCE WITH YOUR REVIEW

Wow! Great job, you've made it this far dear reader. I know that every moment in a caregiver's life is jammed packed, so I congratulate you for your stick-to-it attitude! As you keep reading, you will certainly be rewarded in several ways.

Would you help someone you've never met, even if you never got credit for it? Who is this person, you may ask? They are like you. People who want to make a positive difference in their dementia person's life, and their own life too. They just need some guidance but are not sure where to look. Books with 5-star reviews stand out as a beacon for guidance.

My mission is to make The Dementia Caregivers Bible accessible to everyone who needs it. Whatever I do stems from that mission. The only way for me to accomplish that mission is by reaching... well...everyone.

This is where you come in. Most people do, in fact, judge a book by its cover (and its reviews). So, here's my ask on behalf of a struggling, exhausted caregiver that you've never met.

Please help those people find this resource by leaving a positive and honest review on Amazon. The review is a gift that keeps on giving to many who are hurting. Your gift costs you no money and less than 90 seconds to make a real change in someone's life, forever. Your review could help:

...one more family to put aside their differences and help the one with dementia

...one more person to keep their paying job by having a steady support care team outlined in this book

...one more dementia patient to find a bit more peace and joy in their time left on earth

...one more year for the DP to stay at home without needing to be placed in a facility yet

...one more relative to get the much-needed practical advice to be a better caregiver

...one more day of rest and respite rather than burnout, to continue longer

...one more life to know the transcendent glory of God in hard circumstances

To get that 'feel good' feeling and help this person for real, all you have to do is...and it takes about 90 seconds... leave a review.

Simply scan the QR code with your camera open on your smart phone. It will show a pop-up link to tap and take you directly to the Amazon site. All you'll need to do is start typing! Or you can go directly to Amazon Books.

Thank you from the bottom of my heart. Now, back to our regularly scheduled programming.

- Your grateful author, Kara

PS - Fun fact: If you provide something of value to another person, it makes you more valuable to them. If you'd like goodwill & gratitude straight from a fellow caregiver and you believe this book will help them - send this book their way. I know I have as well.

PART II

"Precious in the sight of the Lord is the death of His saints."

- Psalm 116:15

EXERCISE FOR THE PERSON WITH DEMENTIA & THE CAREGIVER: KEEPING THE BODY & MIND ACTIVE

There are ample physical, mental, and stress reduction benefits of regular exercise for individuals with dementia and their caregivers as well. Doctor Rudy Tanzi mentions exercise and how to "shield" the Alzheimer's brain or for the one without the disease. The link is found in Chapter 30.

In its myriad forms, physical activity acts as a balm with preventative byproducts for both body and mind, mitigating the bodily and psychological impacts of sustained caregiving. The stamina that comes from regular exercise transcends mere physical health; it can also impact one's emotional well-being. Embedding physical activity into a demanding schedule requires a steadfast commitment equal in importance to sleep, meals, and medications. Even brief intervals of movement, be it stretching, utilizing chair fitness, or brisk walks, can inject a surge of energy and clarity into the caregiver's day, proving that the quantity of time is not as important as the quality of the activity chosen.

Physical activity is a therapeutic endeavor that helps you both get a good night's sleep. Physiologically, engaging in physical activity offers a cascade of benefits, fortifying the heart, invigorating circulation, and bolstering the musculoskeletal framework, thus warding off more physical decline. Emotionally, exercise rhythms serve as a mood stabilizer, instilling a sense of achievement, confidence, and happiness. Fitness with others fosters moments of joy and connection beyond the confines of dementia. Exercise raises our feel-good neurotransmitters like dopamine and is a clinically proven depression reducer, equal to or better than antidepressant drugs alone. When music is added, it makes exercise enjoyable; thus, it is not a chore for the DP or the caregiver.

"God has chosen the foolish things of the world to put to shame the wise, and God has chosen the weak things of the world to put to shame the things which are mighty;" - I Corinthians 1:27

20.2. Recommendations for safe and enjoyable exercises include walking, gentle stretching, balance activities, strength training, and swimming for some individuals. Suitable exercises for the DP demand a keen sensitivity to the individual's current state of being. Integrating physical activity into daily rituals—be it a morning stretch to greet the day or an afternoon stroll through nature—transforms exercise from an isolated task into an integral aspect of life's rhythm. This practice allows for various activities to be in harmony with the DP's ability and energy levels to ensure that exercise remains a source of pleasure rather than a source of stress. Begin with gentle stretching for flexibility. Walking on a flat or hilly surface is the first and often easiest exercise to implement. Put their headphones on or earbuds in and set off on a little adventure. I suggest only the DP wears them, as you must stay alert and undistracted for safety. Be willing to pause and enjoy nature or people along the way. Balance activities like Pilates are meticulously designed to fortify the body's equilibrium systems and provide a buffer against falls, ensuring that the pursuit of physical activity doesn't accidentally cause harm. Pilates for seniors reduces joint pain, strengthens the core muscles to add stability and prevents the likelihood of falls. Going to a gym is unnecessary; all that is needed is a wall to incorporate Pilates, a cushioning mat, and a supportive set of sneakers. Pilates are versatile, low impact, mostly stretching poses. This contributes to increased oxygenation and helps release built up stressors. (ten Bosch, 2024)

If you only have a small space, turn up the music or YouTube video and move. The idea is to exert the cardiovascular system a little, which is crucial for maintaining balance, ensuring that all body tissues receive adequate oxygen and nutrients, thus effectively removing waste products. It regulates body temperature and pH levels, protecting the body through immune responses and blood clotting mechanisms. Its proper functioning is vital for overall health and well-being.

"For bodily exercise profits a little, but godliness is profitable for all things, having promise of the life that now is and of that which is to come." - I Timothy 4:8

20.3. If you have a private or a community pool, swimming, and water aerobics with or without weights are excellent choices for gentle fitness and fun. Either of you, or both, may want to join an Aqua Aerobics class at a community center. These have low-impact benefits for those with painful arthritis because of the buoyancy effect: it reduces joint stress and pounding. Sitting on the lower steps up to the waist (holding the step bars if needed) and doing flutter kicks in the water is a good activity for those who can't swim for whatever reason. To improve balance and coordination, resistance training, water walking, and core strengthening can be accomplished in the water with or without water weights, kickboards or resistance bands, etc. One's body weight is enough to produce great results. However, I do suggest water shoes for better traction.

Though there are certainly dangers with any body of water, if it is your pool, it must be secured with a locked high gate (not just for children) and sensors that immediately cause a loud alert when the water moves. All community pools have a locked gate or a wall around them, but this key must be kept out of reach, or the keypad ID must be kept unknown to your DP. Letting the community guard, HOA, or COA manager know of their dementia is an intelligent step toward security. Your vigilance becomes heightened if you live near an ungated or unwalled body of water, like a lake or river, all year round. Even though it is beautiful, significant danger lurks in the water or thin ice. The best you can do to keep your DP safe is to keep your doors locked and your security alarm on for exiting as well as entering.

"Lord, what is man that You take knowledge of him? Or the son of man that You are mindful of him?" - Psalm 144:3

20.4. Monitor the DP's response to exercise and adjust activities as needed for safety and enjoyment. If the DP used to play badminton, tennis, golf, pickleball, volleyball, etc., trying this activity could engage their muscle memory. Thus, it could be a welcome activity, even for you both. However, they may not be able to do these strenuous activities anymore. More situational awareness is needed during the exercise, and the readiness to adjust activities is needed. This, too, becomes a critical element of effective caregiving. Be attentive to discern subtle shifts in their response to physical activity, enabling timely modifications that prioritize well-being and enjoyment. Adjustments may range from altering the intensity of exercises to modifying the environment in which they occur to keep exercise fun and productive. If it gets too difficult or frustrating, distract them quickly and offer something else. Keep it fun, keep it free, and keep it fulfilling. Get an inflatable ball and toss it to one another, try a hula hoop or modify jumping jacks. For musical fun try the 90's hit song "Macarena" by the Spanish duo Los del Río or the "Cha Cha Slide" by DJ Casper that instructs as you go. Whatever you try, recognize the bodily limits and still have fun. As learned in Chapter 12, music is a memory enhancer, so this suggestion has dual benefits.

Physical exercise is a reminder that even in the face of cognitive decline, the body's capacity for movement and the heart's capacity for joy remain. The benefits of exercise—physical, mental, and emotional—form a trifecta of reasons that underscore the importance of this practice, not just for the individual with dementia but for the caregiver as well. Through the thoughtful selection and adaptation of exercises, caregivers can ensure that these activities provide a source of strength, relief, and connection, enriching all who join in.

"Or do you not know that your body is the temple of the Holy Spirit who is in you, whom you have from God, and you are not your own?" - I Corinthians 6:19

"And David danced before the Lord with all his might, wearing a priestly garment." - II Samuel 6:14. NLT

21

A GUIDE TO EASIER ACTIVITIES OF DAILY LIFE (ADL); CREATING A DEMENTIA-FRIENDLY HOME ENVIRONMENT

I n this chapter, the art of simplifying daily activities for dementia patients lies in deconstructing each task into elemental steps, like a chef preparing a complex dish by focusing on one ingredient at a time. This approach not only clarifies the process for the DP but also imbues each step with an essential sense of accomplishment. Each step must be calibrated and verbally identified to relieve fear and confusion. These strategies respect the dignity of the individual while addressing the practical realities of their daily needs.

- Consistency is key. Establish a daily routine for activities like waking up, meals, personal care, and bedtime. A consistent schedule can help reduce confusion and anxiety.
- Divide each activity into easy-to-follow steps. Instead of saying, "Take a shower," break it down into smaller steps like, "Remove your shoes, top, etc." "Turn on the water." "Step in very carefully." "Wet your body." "Apply soap," etc.
- Use visual cues in pictures, diagrams, or written

instructions to guide the DP through each activity step. Create a visual checklist to help them stay on track.

- Offer gentle, simple language and speak slowly. Avoid asking open-ended questions; instead, give specific clear instructions.
- Create a quiet, clutter-free environment to help the person focus on the current task. Reduce background noise and distractions that may cause confusion or agitation.
- Model the activity or provide hands-on assistance. Sometimes, people with dementia need to see someone else repeatedly do the tasks before they can do it themselves.
- Encourage the person to do as much as possible independently. Offer assistance when needed but allow them to complete tasks at their own pace and in their own way.
- Offer praise and encouragement for each step completed successfully. Focus on the effort rather than the outcome and celebrate even small achievements.
- Remember that tasks may take longer than usual, and there may be setbacks along the way. Stay calm, patient, and flexible, and be prepared to adapt your approach as needed.
- If you're having trouble helping the person with their ADLs, consider seeking guidance from healthcare professionals, such as Occupational Therapists OT, Physical Therapist PT, or dementia specialists. They can provide personalized strategies and support items.

21.2. Most activities take more time with a dementia patient, thus it is unwise to try to rush them. No one likes to be bossed around, though they often can't remember you showing them the last time. There is a skillful way to get someone to do what is needed; being aggressive and controlling will usually fail. Remind yourself that the disease makes them hesitant or fearful, and they are not resisting you with a devious intention; it is not really about you. Some patience, gentleness, and creativity are required when assisting a DP in doing things they once did alone. What this looks like for your DP may be unique, but everyone likes praise and reassurance.

I have found that clearly speaking the steps and acting them out can really help your DP understand. Above all, make sure you adhere to the DP's previous routine and time of day as much as possible. If these ADLs are random, you will not find consistent cooperation. You may want to add music and use the same song daily for one theme of tasks to initiate a musical memory peg for each set of tasks, then change the song for another set of tasks. Such as music for each meal of the day, or exercise time, or bedtime, etc. The song(s) can be a preemptive audio direction and save valuable time and frustration. After a while, they may know where to go and how to begin when they hear the song. Once again, you will need to recognize the abilities and limits of your DP and adjust tasks accordingly.

"But, beloved, do not forget this one thing, that with the Lord one day is as a thousand years, and a thousand years as one day." - II Peter 3:8

21.3. Include their choices in what to wear on this day. Tell and show them the weather outside, or point to a weather chart you've set up, though they may not understand you, and guide them to choose appropriate clothing. If they are beyond this mentally, give them just two easy put-on and off, comfortable matching choices, along with one pair of underwear, socks, and slip-on shoes. Lay them on the bed and let them pick one outfit. Have clothes with elastic waists and larger arm holes for ease. Eliminate items with zippers, buttons, belts, and shoelaces; Velcro is a favorable substitute. They may not remember what "Put this leg into the left pant leg" means; that direction may be gibberish to them, and you'll need to model it, plus say it. Keep a firm chair or furniture close by to hold onto for balance. If they are yelled at or disrespected, they may shut down altogether. The adage is also true: "You can catch more flies with honey than vinegar." If the DP still knows who they are in the mirror and their cognitive decline is not at the bottom, these steps will still be meaningful to them. If dressing and undressing are regularly met with resistance, it could be arthritis or some other pain, not stubbornness. Make sure they've had their medication to alleviate pain before this step. It could also be an imaginary fear or offense. Recognize that there may be plateaus where the DP appears to remain the same for a period, followed by a sharp decline in any one or more areas.

To always remain effective, you will need a constant recalibration of expectations and approaches to ensure that care remains responsive to the individual's current reality. The caregiver's role transforms into that of an astute observer and investigator. This flexibility ensures that care remains both supportive and empowering, never crossing the boundary into over-assistance or caretaking instead of caregiving. Let them do what they can for themselves, and never take that positive activity from them if it's not done perfectly or quickly enough (unless it's a real emergency). They need to feel this achievement; no matter how small, any success can genuinely elevate their mood.

"That the person of God may be complete, equipped for every good work."
- II Timothy 3:17

21.4. Making the entire home dementia friendly to make ADL safer and more accessible. The following is also for those people with dementia who live alone when they are diagnosed. However, living alone will need to change for their safety at some point in the future when their sound judgment is severely limited. Independence is tightly held for most people, especially singles, who are used to making all their own choices. Once again, the caregiver will need grace, patience, and kindness to suggest or make these changes. When the time comes when they must have a live-in caregiver or move elsewhere to save their life (with a family member or to a facility), then a strategy of calm yet consistent determination must prevail. There will be tell-tale signs they can't live alone, such as:

Isolation depression, falling frequently, insufficient food in the home, losing weight, kitchen fires, not taking their medications, ancillary health problems, wounds or cuts, excessively high water, gas, or electric bills, not paying utility bills resulting in service being cut off, leaving most lights on all day or overnight, losing house keys, getting locked out, getting lost while out, having important things disappear, accidental (embarrassing) exposure, living in filth, hoarding, not removing garbage, inability to manage the pet(s), or not keeping up with a reasonable standard of ADL.

The goal is to balance respecting their independence and keeping them safe and physically well. Hurting their feelings and stirring up anger may be the price you need to pay for keeping them alive until they succumb to the inevitable disease. Better safe than sorry is best for all because that kind of grief is planted deep in regret.

If the DP remains with a spouse in their home, the benefit is that one spouse can become the primary caregiver if they are capable and willing. They can choose wisely what to move, store, sell, or give away to make life easier and less cluttered. The goal is to make the DP's areas minimalistic, less confusing, and less dangerous. Crafting a home environment for the DP where every element is designed to support his/her ability to move confidently and efficiently. Adding grab bars where there are none is a wise safety measure to have installed where they traverse most. This process involves removing obstacles, simplifying layouts, and ensuring safety measures are in place. Simple modifications, such as clearly labeling cabinets, eliminating unnecessary clutter, and using contrasting colors to delineate spaces, can help. You may apply bright glow-in-the-dark tape or LED strips on the floor or at arm height to reduce confusion and enhance navigability, especially at night.

Put away items that are not meant to be dangerous but can become so in the wrong hands, such as a curling iron, hairdryer, laptop computer, or any electronic device that could break or worse, such as being exposed to water, causing shock or death. Others are more obvious, such as knives, electric lighters or matches, some can openers, metal skewers, garlic presses, an electric blender, etc. Always keep the garbage disposal **unplugged** under the sink until you use it. This has been known to be a *favorite toy* for some DP's. These and other items can cause an injury if not used correctly. Designate one locked closet for the items in each room or put childproof locks on drawers and cabinets. It's a lot of work to identify, remove, or secure potential hazards, but their safety is worth it. There are professionals who do this type of work if it's too much for you and your family.

This approach supports the individual's ability to engage with their environment and minimizes the risk of accidents, creating a functional and comforting space. A safe, navigable place makes the comforts of home longer-lasting.

"My people will live in peaceful dwelling places, in secure homes, in undisturbed places of rest." - Isaiah 32:18

21.5. In a world where digital dominance often overshadows the tangible, the value of a hardcopy resource list remains high for many people. This log is a resource and reminder for you to share data with the professionals, as we can all forget during these fast-paced appointments. One tip is to fill a small binder or notebook with their medical history and past or current behavior to communicate to the doctor. Another option for mobility and security is an electronic interactive medical log, designed for caregivers to track appointments, medication changes, records and reactions, etc. It also can become a valuable tool. These digital or physical logs act as a central repository of information, accessible momentarily, to share with new providers, emergency responders or during routine check-ups. It ensures that, regardless of the setting, the care provided to the loved one is informed, consistent, and tailored to their evolving needs. For a paper notebook log, I suggest customization using a pencil when it's temporary, red and black ink pens for critical points, and highlighters to express daily use. If you prefer a digital interactive device, only one of the following must be utilized; having several platform sites or applications is just too confusing. This list is not exhaustive.

- **My Medical**: This app allows users to keep track of their medical history, medications, allergies, and other health-related information.
- **Apple Health**: Apple's Health app allows users to store and track their medical records, including lab results, medications, and immunizations, all in one place.
- **Google Health**: Google Health offers a platform for users to store and manage their health information securely. It

integrates with various health devices and apps to provide a comprehensive view of one's health data.

- **Microsoft HealthVault**: Microsoft's HealthVault is a secure platform for storing and sharing health information. It allows users to upload and manage their medical records, test results, and other health-related data.

- **Medisafe**: While primarily a medication management app, Medisafe also allows users to keep track of their medical records, including doctor's appointments, lab results, and other health-related information.

22

SAFETY FIRST: PREVENTING COMMON ACCIDENTS AND WANDERING

I ntroducing adaptive tools, technology, and practical steps that can assist with daily tasks, promoting independence and safety. A tablet equipped with communication apps bridges the chasm that speech difficulties or inadequate memories may impose, its screen is a canvas for expression and understanding. Wearable devices that track activity and physiological responses offer insights into the health trends of those with dementia, and their data creates a dialogue between caregiver and clinician. Smart home systems, with their capacity to control lighting, temperature, appliances, and locks, provide an environment that is safe and conducive to independence. Each product, selected with discernment, underscores the commitment to care informed by innovation, ensuring that technology serves not as a replacement for the human touch but as an enhancement. Adaptive devices and tools can be heroes in the caregiver's arsenal, offering solutions that help preserve some of the DP's freedom and autonomy. Consider the simplicity of a lever-handled door, which, when replaced with a traditional knob, opens a world of independence for fingers that no longer grasp and turn with ease. However, this will not be beneficial if or when the DP begins to wander away from home. A different approach will need to be implemented then. See the next section on wandering.

Picture the transformative power of a talking watch for someone who has lost track of time, offering them the hour and a measure of control in their daily life. These tools and more, though small in form, carry immense aid for the DP. Some of these may be redundant but are worthy of repetition. Here is a concise, practical, and logical list to ensure the home environment is as safe as possible for your DP, with peace of mind for you:

- **Clear Pathways:** Ensure that pathways throughout the home are clear of clutter, furniture, and other obstacles to prevent tripping hazards. Offer only slippers and shoes with good traction.
- **Good Lighting:** Ensure adequate lighting throughout the home, especially in hallways, staircases, and entrances, to minimize confusion and disorientation.
- **Remove Hazards:** Remove or secure rugs, electrical cords, and other potential tripping hazards. Install grab bars in bathrooms, hallways, and staircases.
- **Labeling:** Label drawers, cabinets, and doors with pictures &/or words to help individuals with dementia quickly identify and locate needed items.
- **Routine and Consistency:** A consistent daily routine can help individuals with cognitive decline feel more secure and confident in their environment.
- **Color Contrast:** Use color contrast to distinguish different areas of the home, such as contrasting colors for walls and floors, to aid navigation. If your wall is white, paint the

baseboards a dark shade. This is like a directional guide for them, as is reflector tape.

- **Move the animal crate** out of the DP's well-traveled path. Attach a bell on their collar to alert anyone of their presence. Keep pets in their own room or space to avoid tripping underfoot.
- **Simple Layout:** Keep furniture and décor simple and minimize changes to the layout to avoid confusion and disorientation.
- **Secure Dangerous Items:** Lock away or remove potentially dangerous items such as cleaning supplies, sharp objects, and medications. Obviously, gun(s) must be secured as well.
- **Easy-to-Use Appliances:** Consider replacing complex small appliances, such as a can opener, with simpler, easy-to-use versions to reduce frustration and confusion.
- **Comfortable and Familiar Spaces:** Create comfortable and familiar spaces within the home where the DP can relax and feel safe in. Have their favorite chair become a go-to safe-zone.
- **Emergency Preparedness:** Ensure the caregiver has delegated an emergency contact person and that emergency exits are clearly marked.
- **Assistive Devices:** Consider using assistive devices such as grab bar handrails, walking aids, keyless entry, and door or pool alarms to enhance safety and security.
- **Regular Maintenance:** Regularly check the home for potential safety hazards and address them promptly, such as trash bags left out, a laundry basket, plants on the floor, or pet toys.
- **Supervision:** When necessary, provide supervision or assistance to ensure the DP's safety, especially in areas such

as the kitchen, bathtubs & showers, or going up or down steps.

- **Help and Guidance:** For personalized recommendations, consult with your caregiver's support group, occupational therapists, or dementia specialists.

22.2. Strategies to prevent wandering include the use of alarms, Global Positioning Service (GPS) devices, and keyless entries. To prevent the DP from leaving the home, it is highly recommended to install a double-sided keyless touchpad lock on the main doors and keep the code from the DP for their safety. Or install a monitored smart lock and deadbolt that alerts you on your phone, though this will awaken you. With any kind of entry needing a code, make sure you give this code to the local fire department and their paramedics in case of emergency so they can get right in. Also, give the code to trusted family members and one or two neighbors.

Add extra security to the sliding glass doors with a strong security pin and/or bar. It may be necessary to hire a technician who can install appropriate security on these kinds of exterior door frames.

Technology offers more than mere alerts; it extends the caregiver's reach through the invisible threads of WIFI and GPS devices, a digital dashboard that maintains connection even as the individual ventures past sight. If your DP is out with you and you happen to lose sight of them as they wandered away, these items will reduce panic and let you know on your smartphone where they are so that they will soon be by your side again.

Here are a few Bluetooth device options: **Apple Air-tag, Tile-Mate Pro, Nerlos Locator, XY Find-It, Chipolo ONE, Cube Key Finder.** These products require you to pair them with your smartphone, tablet or computer to activate the system. They each have a battery life of 1-2 years.

Also, if you prefer; **KeyRinger** uses radio frequency instead of Bluetooth and a smartphone. In case any keys go missing, you may want to put a small key finder (like Apple Air-tag or Tile-slim) on the car and house key rings (purse, wallet, & other items) with an adhesive mount. You'll ask Siri, Alexa, or Google, to see the item's location and/or request the tag to make a sound for you to follow. As mentioned in Chapter 16; *tap this button before you take out the garbage, as your keys may have inadvertently been placed in the garbage can.*

Alarms, sensors, and silent watchers of the night become vital allies in this endeavor to keep the caregiver(s) informed. These discreet yet effective devices alert caregivers to movements that whisper the onset of an unsanctioned journey. If the DP is able to get a car's keys or has an electric vehicle they can unlock, they may take off this way. If they manage to drive away, call 911 as soon as possible to notify the police of the situation. Many states have what's called a "Silver Alert" or a similar system and name. It is displayed on the electronic highway notification boards and through an alert on our mobile smartphones as to whom to watch out for and what vehicle they may be in. It is like an Amber Alert for child abduction but is for memory-impaired citizens. If your DP has a hidden Air-tag or Tile-mate on them, you can assist the police in locating your escapee.

These GPS tracker devices, worn as pendants or on the wrist. These serve as both beacon and tether, ensuring that even when disoriented, the DP is never truly lost. You can choose from many styles and types of digital monitors available on the market with various attachments.

You may like to use one of these:

- **Jiobit Tracker**
- **iTraq Nano**
- **AngelSense Assistive Technology Watch**
- **Feel Tranquil GPS Watch**
- **SecuLife SOS GPS Tracker**
- **Theora Connect wearable**
- **Apple Watch, Samsung Galaxy Watch, Garmin Watch, Fitbit, Fossil Gen 6, etc.**
- **TileMate; TilePro, TileSlim or TileSticker**

Consider any of these or make their cell phone trackable whether the phone is off or on. Modern cell phones already have a Bluetooth location service. Enable the "find my" feature on the Apple or Android phone to turn on this tracking. Make sure they have straps attached to the phone that go over the head and hang like a necklace, or an armband, to help ensure it is with them, especially when you're out of the house. Add this step to their routine and/or the GPS watch so it will likely be on them. In addition to finding lost keys, purse, wallet etc. these small, easy to hide products help locate people too. Again, you can choose an **Android Samsung Galaxy SmartTag, Apple Air Tag or Tile-pro** type to actually sew into the fabric, put in a wallet, or glue on the item of everyday wear, (jacket, shoes, or purse, etc.) for additional reliability.

Some people with dementia are clever and determined enough to bypass these security and positioning aids. DP's have been known to cut off the straps, take off the necklace or toss the phone etc., so that they can get away undetected. I do want to make it clear that these devices or apps will not keep them at home, they are just tools to identify the area they have wandered to. In this situation it is best to alert authorities and get help in finding them. To minimize the possibility of this, I encourage you to prioritize the entryways and exits of the home as described earlier in this chapter, as well as keeping a location detector device on their person all the time.

22.3. Tips for safely managing medications, including the use of pill organizers and reminders. With dementia and general health care, good medication management can alleviate stress and confusion to ensure the day's dose is taken on time. For organization, blister packs of pre-sorted medications are helpful. Most major pharmacies offer this service for free or a small fee. A very popular one is **Pillpack.com** found on **Amazon Pharmacy**. Other tools available are basic and advanced, as well as electronic pillboxes and dispensers. They can be found online, in most drug stores, or in Walmart. There are pill reminder watches and apps like **Medisafe, MyTherapy**, and **Pill Reminder**. You can also set the reminder on your Apple smartphone and say, "Hey Siri," or use an Android smartphone to say, "Hey, Google" to initiate the reminder. Finally, you can ask your **Alexa**, **Amazon Echo,** or **Google Home,** to audibly remind you when it's time to take the meds. This setup is not difficult, but you may ask a friend for help. These organizers and reminders that chime the passage of time, ensure that medication becomes not a source of distress but a regular ADL. Though it takes a moment to set up, these organizers and reminders will save time and prevent accidents. Other than the occasion of distribution, medication containers must always be kept in a locked cabinet or box.

Apps that keep the home secure, manage medication schedules with precision and gadgets that monitor health metrics in real-time now serve as steadfast allies, becoming extensions of the caregiver's intent.

The simplest item is to order and customize a medical alert ID bracelet with a difficult to remove clasp. Among the available options online are:

- MyMDLife for Alzheimer's patients @ ALZstore.com
- Custom alert ID bracelet by MissNaNa on Amazon
- Road ID Sport Pin Tuck medical ID bracelet @ roadid. com/products/sportpintuck
- Bay Alarm SOS Wristband with push button @ bayalarmmedical.com
- LifeLine watch @ lifeline.com
- Medical Guardian Move smartwatch @ medicalguardian.com
- ADT Health monitored watch @ adt.com/cf/bps/health/
- Mobile Help Classic @ mobilehelp.com/pages/ mobilehelp-wrist-button
- UnaliWear medical alert watch @ unaliwear.com
- If style is an important factor for her try Lauren's Hope Medical ID bracelet and alert jewelry @ laurenshope.com

Depending on the type of device, you will get an alert or a call when they are found, or the device will alert you when there's been a fall. Include your phone number and the DP's memory impairment data in the wristband or bracelet (Mace & Rabins, 2011). Add more information if they take any medications that may interact poorly with other drugs or have a separate bracelet just for this. Adding their address for security may be unwise, as this information could fall into the wrong hands.

Each action of foresight and innovation weaves a thread in the blanket of care, where the DP is not defined by the limitations of their condition but by their boundless intrinsic worth as a human being, by your great love, and by the limitless value God Himself places on each of us.

"Don't copy the behavior and customs of this world, but let God transform you into a new person by changing the way you think. Then you will learn to know God's will for you, which is good and pleasing and perfect." - Romans 12:2 NLT.

23

FINANCIAL PLANNING: SECURING THEIRS & THE FAMILY'S FUTURE

Having organized, easily retrievable documents can lessen the stress related to the DP's many needs to come. If not already in place, I suggest that medical, legal, life insurance, identity proofs like a birth certificate and military records, tax returns, SS card, Passport, titles to auto(s), title to the house(s), or apartment, boat, and any other important documents be stored in waterproof, fire-resistant holders or in a safe or safety deposit box off-premises to which you hold the keys to or lock combination. You'll also need to be aware of debts, loans, liabilities, and ongoing ministry or other kinds of regular giving (automatic, too). The ability to make informed decisions under duress is necessary for the caregiver's commitment to vigilant advocacy, ensuring that the rights and needs of those you care for are defended and their predetermined commitments are honored, if possible.

Financial needs associated with dementia care, including potential home care costs, medical treatments, and long-term care facilities, must be identified and consulted. Navigating the economic landscape of dementia care requires an awareness of the various needs and expenses that accompany this condition. The monetary demands across a broad spectrum encompass daily care necessities, medical services outside of coverage, and, potentially, the accommodation of long-term care facilities. Each facet of dementia care brings its own set of financial considerations, from the immediate costs of home adaptations that ensure safety and comfort to the ongoing expenses of medications, therapies, and professional caregiving support. Moreover, when the specter of long-term care is at hand, the choice of quality facilities that offer specialized dementia care, excellent holistic support, and high-security measures often commands substantial fees. Understanding these needs, in their breadth and depth, lays the groundwork for a comprehensive approach to financial planning that seeks to address the present and anticipate the future.

"Lord, you alone are my inheritance, my cup of blessing. You guard all that is mine." - Psalm 16:5

23.2. Creating a financial plan tailored to the requirements of dementia care is like plotting a course through uncharted waters, requiring precision, foresight, and flexibility. This endeavor begins with a meticulous assessment of current assets, casting a wide net to encompass savings, all investments, insurance policies, and potential sources of income, including social security and pensions. Against this backdrop of resources, the caregiver must then juxtapose the anticipated expenses of dementia care, crafting a financial blueprint for current needs with future demands. This plan must remain dynamic and capable of adapting to the evolving landscape of dementia and the financial markets alike. The first step is to gather as much economic data as possible that you can get your hands on. If your DP is still competent enough to help, by all means, let them assist in this endeavor; you be the judge. If they are not, hopefully, you are the primary custodian of these documents and accounts. Knowing the current financial landscape will offer some trajectory options for where you and the DP may be headed.

"For which of you, intending to build a tower, does not sit down first and count the cost, whether he has enough to finish it—." - Luke 14:28

23.3. Financial planning professionals specializing in **eldercare planning** are invaluable. Armed with a deep understanding of the unique financial challenges posed by long-term care needs, these experts offer insights that transcend generic financial advice, tailoring their recommendations to the nuanced demands of dementia care. The benefits of such counsel are manifold, offering strategic financial planning and guidance on navigating the insurance industry, government benefits, and tax implications related to long-term care. Engaging with a financial planner specializing in eldercare is an act of due diligence, a step that ensures the financial strategy in place is robust, responsive, and aligned with the caregiver's and the person with dementia's best interests.

Tips for protecting assets and investments to ensure long-term financial security for both the caregiver, if they are the spouse or inheritor, and the DP. An excellent financial planner or elder attorney will consider your comfort around risk tolerance, time horizon, and the specific financial landscape of dementia care when it becomes relevant. Suppose you do not have long-term care insurance, a hybrid policy, or a health savings account. In that case, you must seek advice from an experienced estate planning or elder law attorney as soon as possible. Asset protection extends into the legal realm, necessitating measures such as establishing irrevocable trusts or annuities to shield assets from being wholly consumed by long-term care costs. These steps must be taken several years in advance by state-specific laws. Your attorney can provide specific guidance on this matter. This protective stance is not merely a financial maneuver but a bulwark against future uncertainties, ensuring that the financial legacy crafted over a lifetime is preserved to the greatest extent possible. Engaging with financial professionals specializing in eldercare, with knowledge of changing Medicare and Medicaid laws and strategies, is a prudent approach to asset protection.

If real estate is involved, there is a new niche of professionals exclusively within the US real estate market firm, Keller Williams. Top agents have been trained & certified with specialized knowledge of incredibly useful and needed skills to help families build, preserve and transfer wealth by using IRS codes to lawfully **eliminate** or minimize capital gains taxes. This designation is called *Real Estate Planner* (REP). Payment of capital gains taxes are **not** inevitable. Before you sell a property, I strongly recommend that you arrange a strategy session with a KW Real Estate Planner to discover the benefits for the DP and/or the one who has the POA. That investment of time could save tens of thousands to hundreds of thousands of dollars which could then be put to better use for the DP's care. This guidance may also even prevent family disputes. Contact the creators of this beneficial program in Hawaii, ihara@iharateam.com to find a REP in your area. So far REP is only available in the U.S., though KW is worldwide.

"Therefore, everyone who hears these words of mine and puts them into practice is like a wise man who built his house on the rock. The rain came down, the streams rose, and the winds blew and beat against that house; yet it did not fall, because it had its foundation on the rock." - Matthew 7:24-25. NIV

24

ADVANCED CARE PLANNING

E ssential legal documents that should be in place, including wills, durable power of attorney (POA), and advanced healthcare directives. A will, the most recognized of these legal instruments, ensures that one's earthly possessions find their rightful heirs according to wishes articulated in clearer times. It includes guardianship designations for minor children or dependents and names the executor of the will whose job is to manage and settle the estate. It is not morbid to have these prepared; they are both loving and practical. A will is the final word from beyond, a testament that speaks when we no longer can. It can include smaller personal items, individual praises or admonitions, instructions for a memorial service, etc. Meanwhile, the POA vests authority in a trusted individual, granting them the power to act on financial and legal matters when one's own voice falters under the weight of dementia. It may or may not be the caregiver, but in many cases it is. Advanced healthcare directives, including living wills and healthcare proxies such as HIPPA authorization, articulate wishes regarding medical treatment, ensuring that one's beliefs and preferences shape decisions in moments of vulnerability. One advanced healthcare directive is a do-not-resuscitate order, DNR. This is generally not wanted if one is healthy and without a life-threatening illness and is valid for the DP in the early and middle stages of the disease. The staff is not giving up on someone with a DNR, but they will not commence with aggressive, painful, excessive medical techniques if the DP in the late stages of dementia stops breathing, for example, which is a part of one's natural death. Many hospice centers have a DNR request or a requirement for admittance. However, this can be ordered by the DP's physician when the time comes.

24.2. A guide for setting up these legal documents, including how to involve legal professionals when necessary. The average cost for a will from a basic will (without complex provisions or trusts) is about $500. A comprehensive estate plan will cost about $5000+. These can go up according to the attorney's experience, geographical location, the size of the estate, and the number of heirs.

The initiation of these documents unfolds in the quiet sanctity of an attorney's office, where legal expertise meets the deeply personal nuances of one's wishes. The process begins with a consultation, a dialogue where fears, hopes, and desires are laid bare. From this confluence of professional guidance and personal reflection, the documents begin to take shape, each clause and provision reflecting one's values and intentions. This step is far better to do earlier in life when dementia is the last thing on your mind. But it is not too late if a basic will is not done already. To some extent, a well-prepared will can save so much trouble later in time, money, and emotions with the stress of state-specific probate. If you have a will, it may need modifications if written long ago. In revisiting these documents, we are reminded of their role not as static artifacts but as dynamic instruments that evolve alongside us. This review and update process is not merely a legal necessity but is our commitment to safeguarding the DP's wishes and appropriate family disbursements. It is essential to regularly review and update legal documents to reflect any changes in circumstances, people, or wishes. This process, often coinciding with significant life events or at predetermined intervals, ensures that the documents reflect the current reality. Drafting these documents is a collaborative bridge between the legal mind and the human heart. It culminates in the solemnity of signatures, where ink meets paper to seal commitments and confer authority. The involvement of legal professionals ensures that the documents stand not only as expressions of intent but as unassailable instruments recognized by the law. Be forewarned, family attorneys wind up with much of the proceeds if there is no will and the parties do not agree on divisions within the estate.

"A good man leaves an inheritance for his children's children." - Proverbs 13:22

24.3. Strategies for discussing legal wishes and decisions with family members, ensuring clarity, and reducing potential conflicts. Conversations about legal wishes and decisions with family members often unfold in the living room, where the familiarity of surroundings softens the weight of the topic. The process begins with invitations for the family (and other loved ones, or faithful employees, etc.) to understand and honor the choices made by and for the DP. In these dialogues, transparency is preferred, though not in harsh sounding or cruel terms. In cultivating an atmosphere where questions are welcomed and concerns are addressed, it may be best to include the DP, especially if they are in the early stages, as it is usually their future care at stake here, not just tangible property.

A family meeting is about building consensus and weaving a collective understanding that can support the decisions made should they need to be enacted. If there is much disagreement, an arbitrator or mediator may be required to referee the emotions and opinions of certain family members. In crafting a legal foundation for dementia care, the meticulous preparation of essential documents offers not just protection but peace of mind.

As an additional note, in Chapter 3, I found that *30% of caregivers die before their dementia person does*. With this in mind, it is also compassionate and wise to get the primary caregiver's affairs in order, if not already done so. Along with the legal, medical, financial, etc., and last wishes, it is merciful to provide some training to the person who will take over the caregiving task for your DP. Of course, this person must be fully aware of this potential commitment and in agreement with it in case they are ever called upon to fill this role. If this person has been around fairly often and you've left detailed notes, directions, files, and resource lists, the transfer should be less complicated for all concerned.

"For God has not given us a spirit of fear, but of power and of love and of a sound mind." - II Timothy 1:7

25

HANDLING COMPLEX CHALLENGES, INCLUDING HALLUCINATIONS AND DELUSIONS

Unfortunately, paranoia and hallucination symptoms may surface in the latter stages. These manifestations, far from mere quirks of an aging brain, are the mind's response to the confusion and fear sown by the erosion of cognitive faculties. Paranoia, with its roots burrowing deep into the psyche, transforms benign intentions and familiar faces into perceived threats, leading to a fortress mentality where the individual feels besieged on all sides. The impact of these symptoms transcends the individual, sending ripples through the caregiving environment team. Visual and auditory hallucinations further blur the lines between the concrete world and the surreal or fantasy world, creating a strange landscape where they are indistinguishable. It can be shocking to hear your otherwise modest and respectable DP blurt offensive or harsh language. This is, again, the disease talking; the disease has removed the suppression filter, and thus, ugly or vulgar thoughts sneak out. Dementia is not from God, so it reveals its authorship in these episodes. It is heartbreaking to see two distinct personalities. The beloved, godly apostle Paul expresses this typical juxtaposition, though he explains a human condition, **not** necessarily a dementia condition:

"For we know that the law is spiritual, but I am carnal, sold under sin. For what I am doing, I do not understand. For what I will to do, that I do not practice; but what I hate, that I do. If then, I do what I will not to do, I agree with the law that it is good. But now, it is no longer I who do it, but sin that dwells in me. For I know that in me (that is, in my flesh) nothing good dwells; for to will is present with me, but how to perform what is good I do not find. For the good that I will to do, I do not do; but the evil I will not to do, that I practice. Now if I do what I will not to do, it is no longer I who do it, but sin that dwells in me." - Romans 7:15-20.

*"But thanks be to God, who gives us the **victory** through our Lord Jesus Christ."* - I Corinthians 15:57.

25.2. It is of utmost importance to seek professional guidance for managing paranoia and hallucinations, including medication management and therapeutic interventions. Treading the fine line between managing symptoms at home and seeking external intervention requires keen observation through the caregiver's intimate understanding of their condition. The decision to seek professional guidance by recognizing that paranoia and hallucinations, with their roots tangled in neurological decline, often necessitate a level of intervention that exceeds your ability. This pursuit of professional assistance is a multi-pronged strategy, encompassing consultations with neurologists to explore the potential for medication adjustments that temper the extremities of symptoms without dulling the individual's connection to the world.

Professionals and caregivers will practice therapeutic interventions, such as those mentioned above, using genuine empathy, validation therapy, gentle reorientation, visual cues, and distraction with redirection. When the episodes become burgeoning and with heightened power, fear, and anxiety, it is time to add a professional to the caregiving team. They may prescribe antipsychotic medications, anxiolytics, and antidepressants, along with therapeutic interventions that build a stronger safety net tailored to the unrelenting progression of the disease. Many professionals will recommend transferring the DP to a facility that is trained and equipped to handle this difficult scenario best. *"God grant me the serenity to accept the things I cannot change, courage to change the things I can, and the wisdom to know the difference."* This serenity prayer is for any and all who need divine direction and peace.

25.3. Communication strategies that can help reassure and support your loved one without reinforcing hallucinations or paranoia. The art of communication in these circumstances is a little different, requiring extra empathy and discernment. If they are not engaging in violent actions, speaking calmly but loudly and taking their face into your hands to ensure direct eye-to-eye contact is important. Say things like, "It's ok, I'm here," "What do you need?", "Let's find your pillow" (or whatever calming item typically brings comfort). It may be helpful to say things to distract them, such as, "Did you see this beautiful rose bush out the window?" or "I'm so excited for you, today is music day!" When addressing hallucinations or paranoia, the caregiver's words become the gentle hands that soothe, acknowledging the fear without legitimizing the delusion, yet do not openly confront it either. If they believe something that is not true, openly denying it makes them even more fearful and agitated. The goal is to offer reassurance without trying to erase their experience. Use phrases that validate the person's feelings while gently steering them towards safety, such as, "I see this worries you; I'll take care of it," or "I understand your feelings; let's see what's going on." These kinds of statements meet the dual goals of acknowledgment and guidance.

Hallucinations are not always fearful, so it does no good to reason with the person that it really is not snowing outside in August or that their late father is cooking dinner in the kitchen. All you can do is comfort and redirect them. Never directly challenge what they "see". If the hallucination is horrific, do not add panic to what they think they see. Gently reassure them you are opposing the enemy, and they don't need to. Act it out to show them you are subduing the fearful entity if necessary. If they want to, it may be best to let them walk it out with you or an attendant by their side to "disarm" what is so alarming to them. This is not the time to use force unless they are violent or aggressively trying to rush outside; unless they think the attacker is inside, then it is alright to take them away from the imagined intruder inside. A lot of patience, creativity, and flexibility are required. This is certainly not the time to raise your voice in aggravation or join the hysteria. Remain calm, remember self-control, and be the thermostat, not the thermometer, as described in Chapter 5.

"Peace I leave with you, My peace I give to you; not as the world gives do I give to you. Let not your heart be troubled, neither let it be afraid." - John 14:27

25.4. Ways to create a safe and supportive environment that minimizes triggers for paranoia and hallucinations. Providing a serene sanctuary to minimize triggers that initiate an episode is smart. Begin with this: if they are agreeable enough, literally hold them in a bear hug for comfort and assurance until they feel calmer. Delicately put the calming item over their eyes and ask if the vision is gone. Then, eliminate any obvious possible issues. Mirrors have been known to reflect false, frightening images. It may be best to eliminate them for the time being. Close the blinds if that is where distractions are, close the curtains or verticals, turn off the TV, and play calm music. Lead them to their comfortable, safe-zone chair. I used to pray over this space and tell the DP that no harm could come to them in this chair; it was surrounded by mighty angels who guarded her/him.

I use this verse from Psalm 91: "For He shall give His angels charge over you, to keep you in all your ways. In *their* hands, they shall bear you up, lest you dash your foot against a stone." You may want to print this out and leave the verse nearby, even on the wall. This space is their pre-established go-to safe zone with no (or less) misunderstood clutter, no noise levels that might overwhelm or confuse, and ensuring lighting is bright, even, and comforting to avoid shadows. I have seen this safe-zone chair often disable or weaken the frightening episode. If you have a two-story (etc.) home, have a second safe zone upstairs.

For paranoia, the emphasis shifts towards predictability and routine, creating a rhythm to daily life that is grounded in a constant world of flux. Personal items that serve as touchstones of reality are strategically placed, offering tactile and visual items that ground the DP in the familiar. Try and redirect them toward the Memory Box (Chapter 16). This environment, balanced between the need for stimulation and the need for tranquility, is where safety and comfort are forged. Be aware that too much stimulation can often have a negative effect.

"The name of the Lord is a strong tower; the righteous man runs into it and is safe." - Proverbs 18:10

26

WHEN HOME CARE IS NOT ENOUGH: EXPLORING OPTIONS

Recognizing the signs that indicate home care may no longer be sufficient for the DP and the caregiver. Other than the DP's mental state, medical reasons, such as an ongoing illness or unmanageable physical problems, may necessitate a move. In the continuum of care for individuals with dementia, a pivotal moment arrives when the familiar setting of the home, once a safe place of comfort and security, no longer suffices in meeting the round-the-clock needs of the DP. This realization, often gradual and reluctant, is marked by both subtle and stark signs. Your keen observation and holistic reflection help crystallize the need to transition to a new setting designed to provide a higher level of structured support and specialized care.

These milestones may indicate the need to transition:

- **Severe memory loss with the inability to express needs**
- **Increased confusion** and **disorientation**
- **Aggressive** or **belligerent behavior**
- **Increased hallucinations** and **delusions.**

- **Debilitating depression**

Accompanying factors may be present, too, such as:

- **Tenacious isolation**
- **Frequent falls**
- **Too many preventable household accidents**
- **Decline in personal hygiene**
- **Nutritional difficulties**
- **Unwillingness** or **inability** to **swallow medications or food**

At this stage, my DP would have a fit if I tried to offer her help with undressing and washing in the shower. All reasoning with her was gone, the music didn't work anymore, and neither did a new towel, soap, or fancy shampoo. She wouldn't get in the shower even if she smelled to high heaven and was itchy. She was so fearful of the bath, so we always used the shower, and I never left her alone. I would go in with her and use the hand-held spray to expedite the washing. Often, as a last resort, I'd go in my own underwear if I couldn't change into my bathing suit or if it was out of reach. But when I saw that managing her was too much, because, in addition to screaming, she slapped me with a rough push. I think she imagined something entirely delusional or inappropriate, which broke my heart. Of course, I never returned the physical aggression, but when she saw me wince and even cry, she calmed down and looked like she felt remorse. I knew then that I needed far more help than I could give for her sake and mine.

"My flesh and my heart may fail, but God is the strength of my heart and my portion forever." - Psalm 73:26

26.2. An overview of the different care options available for early, middle, and end stages, other than the DP entirely on their own or a live-in arrangement. The landscape of care beyond the home offers several options, each tailored to varying levels of need, stages of dementia, and affordability considerations. Private facilities are not always monitored by oversight entities, yet many are better and more intimate than large corporation-run places. **Aplaceformom.com** can help to evaluate your local facilities and give you recommendations to compare them.

Among the corporate or private options are:

- **Independent Living Facility, ILF**
- **Adult Care Living Facility, ACLF**
- **Continuing Care Retirement Community, CCRC**
- **Assisted Living Facility, ALF**
- **Skilled Nursing Facility, SNF**
- **Specialized Memory Care unit**
- **Psychiatric Hospital**
- **Hospice services**

An ACLF houses many of these specialized care programs on a campus or in different buildings' wings. CCRCs are similar in structure, but they may have private homes or apartments as well as private clubs, groups, life-affirming programs, etc. Both options have a patient transition capacity. As the person requires more care, they can transfer into units that deal with a higher level of needs. This benefit makes the transition less disruptive and often less frightening.

An ILF is just that, mostly independent. They offer apartments or homes for residents who are still largely independent but may need some assistance with daily activities. It is an option for those with early-stage dementia. The next step past an ILF is an ALF, which emerges as a viable choice for those in the earlier to middle stages, offering a blend of independence with assistance in ADL

(Chapter 21) and medical oversight. For those requiring intensive medical care or rehabilitation and continuous supervision, an SNF stands ready and equipped with the resources and expertise to manage complex health issues alongside dementia. Finally, Memory care units specializing in the nuances of dementia care provide an environment engineered to address the unique challenges of cognitive decline, featuring secured areas to prevent wandering and staff trained in the latest dementia care techniques. For behaviors that exceed the capabilities of an SNF or a Memory Care place, or when the interventions repeatedly fail, the physician may refer them to a Psychiatric Hospital for their safety as well as the staff's. Hospice services can go to wherever the patient currently resides or transfer to a specific Hospice unit, often in or near a hospital.

Your insurance policy details or your Medicare plan coverage can be ascertained by a call to or meeting with your local insurance agent. Navigating this array of options includes understanding the DP's current needs, anticipated progression, financial status, and insurance coverage. It unfolds through your and other's research, consultation, and heartfelt consideration of what environment will best nurture their well-being and advanced directives. A face-to-face visit to any of these facilities in your area is a must. Some are tawdry and not what they appear to be online. Many of these facilities mentioned above have smaller, privately owned and operated options, both for-profit and non-profit. There are Church affiliated or community non-profits (often less expensive) that may sound like a viable option, but always check them out, too. Some of the corporate facilities have far more resources to offer amenities, more medical staff, and better security measures. No matter where you may prefer, personal recommendations from someone you trust are certainly a welcome factor.

"The salvation of the righteous is from the Lord; He is their stronghold in the time of trouble." - Psalm 37:39-40

26.3. Diligence and discernment are required to evaluate each potential care facility. This process ensures that the chosen environment aligns with the highest standards of care, safety, and respect for the individual's autonomy, quality of life, and proximity. At the heart of this evaluation lies a checklist of critical factors, a guide to probing beneath the surface of brochures and tours to ascertain the true caliber of the facility.

Consideration is given to the:

- Qualifications and training of the staff
- Their expertise in dementia care
- Their ratio to residents
- The attitude of the staff
- Cleanliness of the common areas

These elements directly impact the quality of personalized attention and support provided.

Safety measures are scrutinized, from the adequacy of security to prevent wandering to the protocols in place for medical emergencies. The presence and quality of dementia-specific programs are assessed, seeking evidence of engagement activities that stimulate the mind, nurture the spirit, and honor the individuality of residents.

This checklist, applied with rigor and insight, becomes a tool for selection and advocacy, ensuring the chosen facility reflects the caregiver's commitment to their loved one's care. Location can't be the main criterion; it must be quality. Some places that are close by may not be the best choice. Large corporate-owned companies or smaller private centers often have different care philosophies. The relief in making a wise and loving choice for your loved one is well worth the effort in finding the best place--- for you both.

26.4. This transition endeavor begins well before the move, involving the individual in discussions to the extent possible and preparing them gradually and gently for the change. Dr's. Mace and Rabins tell us that "When people who have dementia move before their illness becomes severe, they are often better able to adjust to their new environment." Furthermore, waiting till they are "too far gone to object" will make the transition more frightful and unstable for your DP to adjust to the strange and unknown surroundings. (Mace & Rabins, 2019, p. 60) This may even trigger episodes of outrage, panic, delusions, or hallucinations. It is a common thought, but it is so true: Timing is everything. But if they are now in a later stage and could not move sooner, keeping your attitude positive, no matter what, and covering the transition in prayer is critically important. Your mindset must be above any sad and fearful feelings you both may harbor. Make it a happy time, like when an adult child goes off to college, part pain, but a big part hope. Remember that you've prepared yourself and your DP for this move for many years. Having the DP visit the place often helps them transition. They may not recall much, but every bit helps. Personal items that carry emotional significance or evoke memories are selected and brought ahead of time to help make the room look familiar. Then, other items will accompany them, transforming the new space into a place that is not scary but comfortable.

Personalizing the new living space transcends decoration; it is an act of anchoring the soul in a sea of change, ensuring that when the individual crosses the threshold into their new abode, they are met with anchors of recognition and warmth. Photographs that echo laughter and smiles, favorite books that whisper of familiar adventures, and cherished mementos that speak of love—all are carefully chosen to represent home in a new setting. There is a genuine possibility that they will like it in their new home with new friends. Socialization, even without talking, is a human necessity. There will now be many options to alleviate boredom and apathy and still maintain their alone time.

On the day of the move, a calm and reassuring presence is essential, as is timing the transition to coincide with the individual's best time of day. Supporting the individual through this period involves an arsenal of reassurances—both spoken and unspoken—that affirm their value, autonomy, and the continuity of their identity despite the shift in their physical surroundings.

Depending on their level of cognition, a "goodbye" may not be wise. You may need to leave while they are distracted by something or someone pleasant to avoid a possible emotional scene and its remaining results left for the staff to deal with. This may be a place for a fib to alleviate anger, anxiety, or panic. These are the days when their forgetfulness protects them from the same pain you may be feeling. Furthermore, introducing new routines and spaces is done with a gentle hand, ensuring that each new step is met with encouragement and the opportunity for the individual to express their feelings and preferences within the set routines offered.

"I will lift up my eyes to the mountains— from whence comes my help? My help comes from the LORD, the Maker of heaven and earth." - Psalm 121:1-2

26.5. As this section of our discussion draws to a close, your work is not done yet; you are now promoted to a restorative role where you find more time to take better care of yourself, knowing your DP is getting the best care possible. Your transition is to a visiting role as their chief advocate, where you keep an eye on your DP's steps on her/his road to eternity. Advocacy in medical settings is akin to translating a foreign language, bridging the gap between clinical knowledge and intimate understanding of the patient's experience. It involves not just speaking on behalf of the loved one but also interpreting their needs and preferences in a context where they may be unable to communicate effectively. This advocacy is grounded in the caregiver's unique insight into the patient's history and current capabilities, enabling healthcare professionals to tailor their approach to the individual's specific needs. It's a dance of diplomacy and determination, where the caregiver's voice becomes the linchpin in the delivery of compassionate and personalized care. It also may mean engaging with the DP in activities provided by the facility, sharing meals, or simply spending quiet time together, reinforcing the bond and providing continuity of care. Through this sustained involvement, caregivers monitor the quality of care and enrich the lives of their loved ones with the invaluable gift of connection.

26.6. Fostering positive relationships with the care facility's staff is pivotal, transforming them from mere providers into partners in care. This relationship is built on mutual respect, open communication, and a shared commitment to the well-being of the DP. A good partnership with the staff begins right away. Even though this transition is for the well-being of both you and the DP, it may be emotionally charged. Recognizing their expertise while sharing insights into your DP's unique preferences and history is best. It will be vital that the staff knows who you are and that you will be the one to run things by and to keep you updated on any changes or situations that need your attention. Since nursing staff and physicians are very busy, it is recommended that you establish at least one contact person on each shift to communicate with directly, this can improve transparency and alleviate confusion. These go-to people should be the kind of professionals who are easy to talk to and are willing to take a few minutes to fill you in on the latest concerning your DP. If you don't have one, create a business-style card with your contact information to hand out to your key contacts and ask for theirs as well. Type their name and number into your phone contacts so you'll see who is calling and answer immediately. See Chapter 21 for log and book ideas.

In the complexities of medical encounters, the advocate's role begins with articulating the patient's needs and history. Bring the interactive or hardcopy medical log suggested in Chapter 21 to avoid wasting the medical personnel's or your time. Add to it in an ongoing manner as needed with the new information garnered while the DP is residing in their new abode. When meeting with staff, take plenty of notes and ask open-ended questions.

"What do people get for all their hard work under the sun?"
- Ecclesiastes 1:3

2 7

EMOTIONAL WELLNESS: COPING WITH GRIEF & GUILT

Exploring the complex emotions of grief and guilt that caregivers often experience both during the caregiving years and after the DP's death. In the quiet hours before the world awakens, or anytime pain swells up, caregivers often find themselves wrestling with the twin specters of grief and guilt. In its multifaceted essence, grief encompasses the anticipatory grief for the loss yet to come and the mourning of the person once known. It may steal moments of satisfaction and replace them with a longing for what was or what might have been. Guilt, its constant companion, whispers incessantly of perceived shortcomings, of words unsaid and deeds undone, of the relentless questioning of decisions made in moments of crisis. Together, these emotions craft an undercurrent that can tug the caregiver into dark depths, where the tenderness of God's mercy and the rational warmth of self-forgiveness seem like distant memories. These are the times to be aware of and seek an alternative trajectory toward hope and acceptance.

"Blessed are the poor in spirit, for theirs is the kingdom of heaven. Blessed are those who mourn, for they shall be comforted. Blessed are the meek, for they shall inherit the earth. "Blessed are those who hunger and thirst for righteousness, for they shall be filled. Blessed are the merciful, for they shall obtain mercy. Blessed are the pure in heart, for they shall see God. Blessed are the peacemakers, for they shall be called sons of God. Blessed are those who are persecuted for righteousness sake, for theirs is the kingdom of heaven." - Matthew 5: 3-10.

27.2. In the shadowed corridors of loss and anticipation, the framework established by Elizabeth Kübler Ross in her creation of The Five Stages of Grief, she and her successors offer a lantern, casting light upon the oft-trodden but uniquely experienced path of grief. (On Death & Dying, 1969. ch 3.) This model delineates grief into five distinct stages: denial, anger, bargaining, depression, and acceptance.

From the moment of diagnosis, caregivers embark on a preemptive journey of grief, a silent procession shadowed by the specter of anticipated loss. This grief, woven into the fabric of daily care, manifests in myriad ways, reflecting the depth of the bond between caregiver and care recipient. It might surface in moments of poignant reminiscence, the quiet observation of incremental declines, or the solitude of contemplation, where the future looms with fear and uncertainty.

The biblical perspective on death and dying offers a lens through which the end of life on earth is a transition, reminding one of the hope and promise of eternal life in heaven. With dementia's drawn-out cruelty, another stage may be present too: that of relief. No more suffering pain, frustration or delusions. They think clearly now and are whole in every way in their new heavenly body! There should be no guilt in feeling relieved, it is entirely accurate. Your DP is finally home where they are eternally safe, gloriously happy, and productive in serving and fellowshipping with Christ Jesus! Nothing could be better; your work for them is done. With this comes rewards that you will one day receive for your earthly efforts of love.

"Then the righteous will answer Him, saying, 'Lord, when did we see You hungry and feed You, or thirsty and give You drink? When did we see You a stranger and take You in, or naked and clothe You? Or when did we see You sick or in prison and come to You?' And the King will answer and say to them, 'Assuredly, I say to you, inasmuch as you did it to one of the least of these My brethren, you did it to Me.' - Matthew 25:37-40.

27.3. In dealing with guilt and grief, an honest and compassionate viewpoint must be initiated. The first step lies in acknowledging these feelings as valid and recognizing that they are universal companions of dementia caregivers. We do not deceive ourselves; we know full well that one out of one people dies, with or without dementia. From this acknowledgment, the caregiver can begin the delicate work of disentangling themselves from the thorns of self-reproach, employing techniques that foster expression, support, and self-compassion. Expressing these emotions, whether through the catharsis of written words in a journal, the release of spoken words in the confidence of therapy or home meditation, the shared understanding found in friends or support groups, or a pastoral visit, all serve as a valve to release the pressure they can exert on the heart. The feelings are real, but they do not have to gain ultimate hierarchy in one's thoughts. The best way to overcome their devastation is by speaking the truth to yourself and overruling their internal battle in your mind with God's perfect word. This is the best antidote to dismantle the pain or set it aside.

"For this corruptible must put on incorruption, and this mortal must put on immortality. So when this corruptible has put on incorruption, and this mortal has put on immortality, then shall be brought to pass the

saying that is written: "Death is swallowed up in victory." "Oh Death, where is your sting? Oh Hades, where is your victory?" The sting of death is sin, and the strength of sin is the law. But thanks be to God, who gives us the victory through our Lord Jesus Christ. Therefore, my beloved brethren, be steadfast, immovable, always abounding in the work of the Lord, knowing that your labor is not in vain in the Lord." - I Corinthians 15: 53-58.

27.4. Healing is not an event but a process that unfurls in its own time, revealing layers of pain and resilience, sorrow, and eventual acceptance. This process does not have a script or a duration. It is unique for each person. Allowing oneself the grace to experience this process without the imposition of timelines or expectations is crucial. The seeds of healing are sown in granting oneself permission to grieve, to feel the full weight of the loss and the frustration of guilt. This healing cultivates a garden where memories can be revisited not as sources of pain but as tributes to the depth of the caregiver's love and dedication to the DP before, during, and after the dementia took them to their forever home. The journey through grief and guilt, marked by its twists and turns, its valleys and peaks, gradually leads to a place where the caregiver can look upon their reflection and see not the shadows of what was lost or what might have been done differently, but the strength that carried them through the darkest nights. When you use the tools to construct a bridge over the chasm of these emotions, a bridge built on understanding eternity and forgiveness of your imperfections, you will gradually return to peace. Then, you can be proud of your accomplishments and tenacity to love and care for "the least of these" to the end. You will one day hear God say:

"Well done, good and faithful servant. You have been faithful and trustworthy over a little, I will put you in charge of many things; share in the joy of your Master." - Matthew 25:21

28

THE DARKEST DAYS BEFORE THE LIGHT

W hether your DP is in a professional memory care facility, with quality nursing care or a psychiatric hospital, during the final phase of dementia, these times can be an extreme challenge to all who interact with them. There comes a time in the DP's life when the severity of advanced Alzheimer's consumes them with a furry of profound memory loss, odd inconsistencies, delusions, aggressions, and helplessness. This time may last a year or two and be dotted with highly unusual or even comical behaviors. The progression and duration of this final stage are influenced by the unique characteristics and health circumstances of the DP. Cesare Pavese said, "The closing years of life are like a masquerade party when the masks are dropped."

The majority of caregivers do not take on this job in their homes because it can be overwhelming and even dangerous. Your once delightful DP will require constant supervision, 24/7. They may lose control of bodily functions, forget where and how to use the bathroom, refuse to shower or take a bath, and be highly resistant to eating. The DP not only may see things that aren't there but may act on them and pick up a "weapon" to fight an invisible, silent enemy. Trying to reason with the DP will not assuage them in the heat of the moment. The DP can become unpredictably aggressive and belligerent one moment and funny or absurd the next. Their nightmares are vivid and quite real to the DP, so they may wake up and engage in verbal and/or physical combat. They may strike out while awake or in their sleep, so they cannot sleep alongside anyone anymore. Sleepless nights are normal during this end stage and can be a real threat to any caregiver's well-being; this sort of behavior becomes nearly impossible for you to handle. These dark, difficult days are only for segments of time for highly skilled professionals.

As the disease progresses, the DP becomes less vocal and animated. The chaotic thoughts that remain are all inside. This inward retreat is often a complex response to the progression of the disease. They have lost the ability to recognize family members, friends, and familiar surroundings. This profound disorientation can lead to isolation because people can no longer connect their current reality with their past experiences. Language skills and emotional connections diminish to the point that trying to express anything is so frustrating and overwhelming that their mind withdraws altogether. Sometimes, the fears and anxiety that remain are so vivid that the DP attempts actions of self-defense toward the generous attempts of others. Eventually individuals may become resigned to their condition. The awareness, even at a subconscious level, of their diminishing capabilities can lead to passive acceptance and a retreat into silence.

"The Lord is near the brokenhearted; he delivers those who are discouraged." - Psalm 34:18

28.2. This story shows that the dark days are unique among dementia patients. Bartholemew was a beloved father and grandfather, a retired engineer who had always been meticulous and precise. His decline due to Alzheimer's disease was gradual but relentless, and by the time he reached his middle seventies, the disease had advanced significantly.

In the final months, Bart's condition deteriorated rapidly. He experienced severe memory loss, confusion, and delusions. He often believed he was back in his childhood home or that his long-deceased parents were still alive. Sometimes, these delusions seemed to provide him comfort, but more often, they led to frustration and fear.

Bart made managing his care increasingly difficult for his family and caregivers. He would become agitated and defiant, particularly with daily activities like napping, bathing, and eating. There were days when he wouldn't recognize his wife, Gwen, which broke her heart. Despite these challenges, she remained his primary caregiver, somewhat assisted by home health aides.

One evening, Bart becomes convinced that strangers are in his house and is adamant about protecting his family from these imagined intruders. His agitation escalates to the point where he yells and tries to barricade the doors. Gwen, unable to calm him down, calls their son, Ken, for help. When Ken arrives, he finds his father trembling and panicking, brandishing a heavy rake as a weapon. Understanding that his father's agitation stemmed from fear, Ken spoke to him in a calm, soothing voice. It took hours, but eventually, Bart's anxiety subsided enough for him to go to sleep. However, at around 4:30 am, Bart awoke and started the loud defensive stance again.

Recognizing that Bart's needs had surpassed what they could manage at home and considering Gwen's dangerous exhaustion, his wife and son made the merciful and wise decision to place him in a specialized memory care facility for as long as finances allowed. The transition was challenging, and Bart sometimes struggled to adapt to his new environment, though his favorite place was in the social room where he could interact with others. Bart liked to be around other people, and they would talk gibberish to one another. After a few weeks, Bart would start yelling at his new friend and initiate a fight over the imagined intruders. This would mean they would need to be separated and relocated. When Gwen and Ken visited, Bart appeared segregated in his room. This was for his well-being as he would escalate the yelling to physical violence. Total isolation is not good, so a secondary plan was implemented. Bart found some peace in the quiet chapel with a few others, but his delusions followed him there. His late father was a former pastor, and Bart vehemently believed his dad was there too. He mentioned his mom would sit by him. When he was accidentally told his parents were already in heaven, this caused fresh, excruciating grief all over again. Getting him out of the chapel for meals and other important routines was difficult because he felt close to his parents there. Since he loved it there and it calmed him down, the staff would do their best to accommodate him there.

Back in his room, Bart was quite suspicious and would often accuse the staff of stealing his things or keeping him prisoner. However, the staff, trained in dementia care, approached him with patience and compassion, showing him the items were safe or using techniques to redirect his attention and calm his fears.

In the final days, Bart's physical health also declined rapidly. Hospice was called and arrived with new staff and solutions. He became bedridden and non-verbal, but the delusions persisted, often manifesting as silent, fearful expressions. The friends, family members, and a few respite caregivers who visited him to say their goodbyes ensured he was never alone, holding his hand, playing his favorite music, and speaking to him gently, even when he couldn't respond.

For weeks, Gwen spent nearly every possible moment by his side, speaking prayers aloud, whispering stories of their life together, and playing his favorite songs. She hoped that somewhere in his clouded mind, he heard comfort in her voice and the sounds of music. Bart passed away peacefully at about 5 am, his hand held by his favorite staff member who came to check in on him. Gwen was ok that she did not observe his passing herself, she was grateful Bart was not alone. All her memories of Bart were of his beautiful life, not his final hours on earth.

28.3. It is therapeutic to allow grief to take its place before, during, and after the DP's death. This poignant song by Glen Campbell and Julian Raymond has become a popular Alzheimer's standard. He co-wrote this song for his beloved wife during his early days of dementia. I suggest you listen to the song and go toward the sorrow rather than deny or stifle it. Though it may bring tears, it will help you heal.

"I'm Not Gonna Miss You"

I'm still here, but yet I'm gone, I don't play guitar or sing my songs.
They never defined who I am, the man that loves you 'til the end.
You're the last person I will love, you're the last face I will recall.
And best of all, I'm not gonna miss you. Not gonna miss you.
I'm never gonna hold you like I did, or say I love you to the kids.
You're never gonna see it in my eyes, it's not gonna hurt me when
you cry.
I'm never gonna know what you go through, all the things I say or do.
All the hurt and all the pain, one thing selfishly remains.
I'm not gonna miss you. I'm not gonna miss you.

29

THE ROLE OF HOSPICE IN END-OF-LIFE CARE

A n overview of hospice care and its services to individuals with dementia and their families at the end of life. At the heart of hospice care lies a 24-hour-a-day sanctuary of compassion and professionalism provided to those nearing the end of their natural life. The soothing and holistic care model, specifically tailored for individuals and their families, emphasizes comfort, alleviating pain, and nurturing emotional well-being rather than pursuing curative treatments. It is not a place for aggressive medical efforts; those are now obsolete and outside of the most minor issues. Services encompass a holistic approach, integrating medical support, pain management, spiritual counseling, and emotional guidance, all delivered where the individual resides, at home, a care facility, or a hospice center. All death-delaying treatments are shelved so the DP is without suffering. In the late final stages of dementia, when the body entirely forgets how to swallow and many other reflexes, the physician will recommend palliative care, not a feeding tube.

I, the author, learned while I served as a Chaplain at our local Hospice that a patient's refusal to eat was an end-stage indicator, a symptom that they were near death. Among other systems, their digestive systems are shutting down. Eating or drinking at this juncture becomes painful and, if forced, could result in further serious medical problems. They will not want food and finally refuse water, even in a small sponge. How long they have varies; it could be a week without food or a couple of days without any fluids, depending on other health factors. Nevertheless, this decision to give nutrition by any means other than eating is entirely up to the professional staff who endeavor to do everything for the patient's comfort scenario.

The essence of hospice care is to afford individuals the serenity to embrace their final days with grace, ensuring their comfort and honoring their wishes, enveloped by the care of a dedicated team of healthcare professionals, counselors, and volunteers. As believers, we know that all souls live forever somewhere; this is just an earthly pause until we meet again in heaven. Keep that in mind when the emotional pain escalates, just thinking of their soon homegoing.

"This day is holy to our Lord. Do not grieve, for the joy of the Lord is your strength." - Nehemiah 8:10

29.2. What are the eligibility criteria for palliative hospice care, and how to determine the right time to consider their services? Eligibility for hospice care pivots on medical evaluations, which ascertain that a person's life expectancy is measured in months, not years, due to the advanced nature of their condition. Most often, it is determined by more than one physician that they have six months or less to live. The determination to shift focus from active treatment to palliative care involves nuanced conversations with medical professionals and what their advanced directive indicates. In hospice care, timing becomes a delicate balance, an endeavor to introduce services at a juncture that maximizes the individual's quality of life, allowing them to savor moments of connection and peace without the exhaustive pursuit of treatments that no longer promise improvement. It was often heard by patients and family alike that they wished they would have sought hospice earlier, sometimes a lot earlier. Hospice is not to be thought of as giving up on the DP, it is not an immediate death sentence, nor is it a morphine-focused tool to silence the DP. It is a comprehensive, comfortable, care-focused professional place led by your love and acceptance of the medical facts.

Fortunately, hospice care is covered by Medicare and Medicaid in all 50 US States and by most private insurance plans. Check your plan to confirm.

29.3. The benefits of hospice care include meals if they can still eat, pain management, emotional support, and assistance with end-of-life planning. Some facilities offer additional therapies, such as music, aroma, pet, and massage. These professionals can bring soothing benefits to the DP by showing compassion and mercy. The embrace of hospice care brings forth many benefits, casting a light of solace and support during a period marked by complexity and emotional depth. Pain management, a cornerstone of hospice care, employs meticulous strategies to alleviate discomfort, allowing individuals to dwell more fully in each moment, to the extent of their status. Beyond the physical, the emotional and spiritual support extended to families and individuals serves as a bulwark against the isolation and despair that may loom in the face of mortality. The chaplain has many duties, such as assistance with offering options for end-of-life planning (coffin burial, cremation, biodegradable tree burial, sea, sky, etc. burials), personal prayers providing clarity and peace, communicating with families' wishes even when the relationships are not quite friendly.

They will advocate for what the DP desired and had documented before the onset of dementia. Your clergy or the hospice chaplain can also conduct a church funeral or "welcome home" service if requested. They can also do the service at another requested place that was important to the DP, like on the beach, a mountain, or at a club they had belonged to etc.

The multidisciplinary approach of hospice care, weaving together various strands of practical and spiritual support, ensures multifaceted care that respects the individual's and family's wishes and upholds their dignity and legacy at life's end.

"I have fought the good fight, I have finished the race, I have kept the faith. Now there is in store for me the crown of righteousness, which the Lord, the righteous Judge, will award to me on that day—and not only to me, but also to all who have longed for his appearing." - II Timothy 4:7-8

29.4. Guidance on navigating the decision-making process for choosing hospice care, including discussing options with health-care providers and family members. The path to hospice care is paved with reflection, dialogue, and, hopefully, the deep wish to honor the individual's needs and desires. One of those conversations is about where. Though it is rare to still be at home at this late stage, your DP will have 24-hour hospice care, as the last days are especially taxing. Often, this professional is the one to tell the family that death is imminent and then when they have passed. Did the DP indicate their wishes of where to pass, or did they say that's up to you? This decision to be at home is fraught with worries as the truth of their end-of-life scenario will happen under your roof and possibly in your bedroom. Though privacy is better and the time to grieve with them is a little longer, the memory of their death will remain in this location, so it is essential to think of the aftermath as well. Plans to sell the home, finish the lease, and move right away may already be settled. Thus, a home death will not be a permanent reminder that is evident every day.

Another thing to consider is how hard and sad it would be to physically transfer them to hospice, if necessary, due to circumstances that are beyond the capabilities of those at home. Many patients die of pneumonia due to dementia. If they are already at hospice or a dementia care facility, it is equipped with many options for palliative care to quickly ease their discomfort. This may be the best location for the DP and for you and your family. The hospice nurses are experts at reading the signs and will summon you when the time is near, within 24 hours or less. Then, the happier memories will remain at your home, somewhat separated by death.

Having choices is a good thing, and hospice is a blessing to so many. The process of family discussions, marked by its emotional intensity and the weight of the decisions at hand, benefits from the guidance of healthcare professionals, counselors, and hospice care teams, who offer their expertise and compassion to guide families through this pivotal moment. The comfort-care model stands as a guide to the value of every moment, seeking to alleviate suffering and nurturing the emotional and spiritual well-being of all involved. The path forward, marked by the continued commitment to understanding, supporting, and honoring those cared for, is set for its last burst of energy across the finish line. You can be confident in this concerning you both:

"And I heard a loud voice from heaven saying, "Behold, the tabernacle of God is with men, and He will dwell with them, and they shall be His people. God Himself will be with them and be their God. And God will wipe away every tear from their eyes; there shall be no more death, nor sorrow, nor crying. There shall be no more pain, for the former things have passed away." - Revelation 21: 3-4.

30

BOOKS, BLOGS, AND RESOURCES
FOR CONTINUOUS LEARNING

Though this book will become your go-to bible, there may be other resources you may want to read as supplemental education. When the world settles into a hush and the weight of responsibility momentarily lightens, the solace found in the pages of these books becomes a sanctuary. These texts, each resonating with the authenticity of shared experience, the clarity of scholarly research, or from a Christian perspective, all have something to offer.

Some resources suggest we can do things to possibly prevent the disease of Alzheimer's. One of these is found at UsAgainst-Alzheimer's.org under the "Our Work" tab. "There are lifestyle changes you can make that can potentially delay or prevent the onset of Alzheimer's, even if it runs in your family. Take the first step today and check out a recent BrainStorm by UsAgainstAlzheimer's podcast session on lifestyle modifications or SHIELD, "**S**leep, **H**andle stress, **I**nteract with others, **E**xercise, **L**earn new things, **D**iet," with Dr. Rudy Tanzi.

"Travelers to Unimaginable Lands: Stories of Dementia, the Caregiver and the Human Brain" by Dasha Kiper & Norman Doidge

Case histories meld science and storytelling.

"Finding Grace in the Face of Dementia" by John Dunlop, MD

A Christian perspective on caring for those with dementia, focusing on finding grace and hope in the journey.

"The 36-Hour Day: A Family Guide to Caring for People Who Have Alzheimer's Disease, Related Dementias, and Memory Loss" by Nancy L. Mace and Peter V. Rabins

In its newest version, this book is recommended by caregiving communities for its comprehensive approach.

"Second Forgetting: Remembering the Power of the Gospel during Alzheimer's Disease" by Dr. Benjamin T. Mast

This book explores how faith and the gospel can strengthen and support caregivers and those suffering from Alzheimer's.

"Treasures in the Darkness: Extending the Early Stage of Lewy Body Dementia, Alzheimer's, and Parkinson's Disease" by Pat Snyder

This book covers Lewy Body Disease with elements of Alzheimer's and Parkinson's disease.

"Creating Moments of Joy Along the Alzheimer's Journey: A Guide for Families and Caregivers" by Jolene Brackey

Focuses on creating meaningful moments and finding joy in caregiving.

"The Dementia Handbook: How to Provide Dementia Care at Home" by Judy Cornish

Provides a practical approach to home caregiving, emphasizing the importance of understanding and responding to the emotional needs of those with dementia.

"Still Alice" by Lisa Genova

It is a novel that provides a deep, empathetic look into the life of a woman with early-onset Alzheimer's, offering insights into those affected by the disease.

"Learning to Speak Alzheimer's: A Groundbreaking Approach for Everyone Dealing with the Disease" by Joanne Koenig Coste

Introduces the "habilitation" approach to caregiving, which focuses on enhancing the quality of life for people with Alzheimer's.

The Caregiver's Voice Website

A blog offering resources, personal stories, and expert advice for caregivers of those with dementia.

AlzAuthors.com Website

A community of authors writing about their experiences with Alzheimer's and dementia, providing diverse perspectives and support through storytelling.

Dementia Care Central Website

It provides practical tips, information on different types of dementia, and resources for caregivers to help them better manage their roles.

30.2. Ongoing innovative education, dementia prevention ideas, and cutting-edge learning for caregivers are ever-evolving and complex; thus, they demand a commitment to continuous learning. This pursuit of knowledge, whether through the latest medical research, innovative caregiving strategies, or insights into the psychological impacts of dementia, is vital. It ensures that the care provided is grounded in the most current understanding, an amalgamation of science, spirituality, and empathy that benefits both caregiver and recipient. Workshops and webinars offered by various esteemed institutions or Christian advocacy groups present opportunities to improve the lives of those who have yet to receive the diagnosis. Maybe one day, hearing those words will be fewer and fewer or not even a death sentence.

"Now may the God of peace Himself sanctify you completely; and may your whole spirit, soul, and body be preserved blameless at the coming of our Lord Jesus Christ. He who calls you is faithful, who also will do it." - I Thessalonians 5:23-25

CONCLUSION

And so, dear reader, we find ourselves at the end of a journey—a journey not just through the pages of a book but through the heart and soul of caregiving. Together, we've meandered through the twists and turns of dementia caregiving, a bewildering and enlightening path scattered with clever ideas amidst our tears and always guided by a beacon of hope and faith.

Our exploration was not just about understanding this condition but about connecting deeply with our loved ones, even as words fail and memories fade. We've talked about the nitty-gritty of daily care, the foresight needed for legal and financial planning, and the absolute necessity of wearing our oxygen masks before assisting others. We've read lists of ideas and strategies to make life better. We've learned about a significant number of tools and gadgets that are available to help along the way.

The heart of our journey together, though, beats in the rhythm of compassion, adaptability, and the unwavering support of objective Biblical truths. This book is to be more than a guide; it's a reference guide to revisit as often as needed, like we do our Bible, and share with those who have just been diagnosed so they too may find the assistance to accompany them on their own dementia journey. The journey is carefully sewn together with strong spiritual threads that create a warm biblical blanket for all who need its comfort.

As I share this journey with you, my hope has been for these pages to light your way, offering solace and strength. May you find in this book a reflection of your own experiences, a validation of your feelings, and a reservoir of strategies to draw upon. Now, I encourage you—no, I urge you—to take these lessons to heart. Reach out to those support networks; they're waiting to hold you up. Prioritize your well-being, physically, emotionally, and spiritually. The strategies and stories shared here are your tools; use them well. Embrace the Word of God, where you'll find a strong tower to run to and a deep well with living water of hope.

In closing, I want to leave you with confidence and courage for the day. This path of caregiving, marked by love and faith, is both a challenge and a privilege. With the right tools and a heart full of compassion, you can provide quality care without losing sight of your well-being. Remember, amidst the trials, there are moments of profound joy and connection to be found. Hold onto, cherish, and record those moments, and let them fuel your journey forward. Refuse to let your loved one's dementia take away your positive and plentiful memories of them.

May you walk this path with your head held high, your spirit supported by community, and your heart open to the encouragement and accomplishment that caregiving with others can bring. You are not alone. With family, friends, and those whom you have yet to meet but will come to love like family, let love and faith be your guides as you face the challenges and the silly moments of humor to find ample endurance for the journey.

With all my heart, I wish you peace, power, and endless love, but the greatest of these is love.

- Warmly, Kara

REFERENCES

Administration for Community Living, National Alzheimer's and Dementia Resource Center, & RTI International. (n.d.). *Emergency Preparedness Toolkit for People Living with Dementia.*

Alive inside—A story of music and memory. (n.d.). Alive Inside. http://www.aliveinside.us

Alzheimer's and hallucinations, delusions, and paranoia. (2017, May 17). National Institute on Aging. https://www.nia.nih.gov/health/alzheimers-changes-behavior-and-communication/alzheimers-and-hallucinations-delusions-and

Alzheimer's Association. (2024). Alzheimer's Association. https://www.alz.org

Bhargava, Y., & Baths, V. (2022). Technology for dementia care: Benefits, opportunities and concerns. *Journal of Global Health Reports, 6,* e2022056. https://doi.org/10.29392/001c.39606

Bible verses about strength to turn to in difficult times. (2024, June 28). Country Living. https://www.countryliving.com/life/g31990757/bible-verses-about-strength/

Britt, K. C., Boateng, A. C. O., Zhao, H., Ezeokonkwo, F. C., Federwitz, C., & Epps, F. (2023). Spiritual needs of older adults living with dementia: An integrative review. *Healthcare, 11*(9), 1319. https://doi.org/10.3390/healthcare11091319

Burer, M. H. (Ed.). (1996). *New testament: New english translation; novum testamenum graece; english text and notes the net bible; greek text and critical apparatus nestle-aland, novum testamentum graece, 27th edition.* Dt. Bibelges.

Campbell, K. (2020). *Gentle on my mind: In sickness and in health with Glen Campbell.* Nelson Books, an imprint of Thomas Nelson.

Caregiver forum and support group—Agingcare. Com. (n.d.). https://www.agingcare.com/caregiver-forum

Center, L. I. A. and D. (2019, April 22). Adaptive devices for persons with dementia. *Long Island Alzheimer's and Dementia Center.* https://www.lidementia.org/adaptive-devices-dementia/

Chalk, J. (1967). Eight steps to christlikeness. *Herald of Truth Documents.* https://digitalcommons.acu.edu/hot_docs/37

Chamine, S. (2016). *Positive intelligence: Why only 20% of teams and individuals achieve their true potential and how you can achieve yours* (1st ed). Greenleaf Book Group Press.

Changes in intimacy and sex with dementia | banner health. (2023, February 8). https://

www.bannerhealth.com/healthcareblog/teach-me/changes-in-intimacy-and-sex-with-dementia

Cloud, H., & Townsend, J. S. (1992). *Boundaries: When to say yes, how to say no to take control of your life* (Updated and expanded [edition]). Zondervan.

Coping with agitation, aggression, and sundowning in alzheimer's disease. (2024, July 17). National Institute on Aging. https://www.nia.nih.gov/health/alzheimers-changes-behavior-and-communication/coping-agitation-aggression-and-sundowning

Dementia. (n.d.). https://www.who.int/news-room/fact-sheets/detail/dementia

Dementia and alzheimer's disease. (n.d.). *DR. TOM ROSELLE, DC.* https://www.drtomroselle.com/podcast/dementia-and-alzheimers-disease/

Dunlop, J. (2017). *Finding grace in the face of dementia.* Crossway.

Fantasia, C. (2019). *In the lingering light: Courage and hope for the alzheimer's caregiver.* NavPress.

Forbes, D., Forbes, S. C., Blake, C. M., Thiessen, E. J., & Forbes, S. (2015). Exercise programs for people with dementia. *The Cochrane Database of Systematic Reviews, 2015*(4), CD006489. https://doi.org/10.1002/14651858.CD006489.pub4

Goldy-Brown, S. (n.d.). Durable power of attorney | what is a durable power of attorney? *SeniorLiving.Org.* Retrieved April 20, 2024, from https://www.seniorliving.org/finance/estate-planning/power-attorney/

Holy bible: New living translation, burgundy, bonded leather, deluxe text edition, indexed. (1996). Tyndale House Publishers.

Hospice improves quality of care in patients with dementia | uc san francisco. (2022, June 3). https://www.ucsf.edu/news/2022/06/423066/hospice-improves-quality-care-patients-dementia

How to create a dementia memory box. (n.d.). Relish. Retrieved March 24, 2024, from https://relish-life.com/en-us/blogs/articles/how-memory-boxes-bring-joy-to-those-living-with-dementia

How to make your home dementia friendly. (2023, August 18). Nhs.Uk. https://www.nhs.uk/conditions/dementia/living-with-dementia/home-environment/

How to use mindfulness to help with caregiver stress and burnout. (2022, March 9). TheKey. https://thekey.com/learning-center/how-to-use-mindfulness-to-help-with-caregiver-stress-and-burnout

Ingram, C. (2015). *The invisible war: What every believer needs to know about Satan, demons, and spiritual warfare.* Baker Books, a division of Baker Publishing Group.

Kiper, D. (n.d.). *The heartbreak and hazards of alzheimer's caregiving.* Scientific American. Retrieved July 28, 2024, from https://www.scientificamerican.com/custom-media/davos-alzheimers-collaborative/the-heartbreak-and-hazards-of-alzheimers-caregiving/ (https://www.davosalzheimerscollaborative.org)

Kurtgöz, A., & Edis, E. K. (2023). Spiritual care from the perspective of family caregivers and nurses in palliative care: A qualitative study. *BMC Palliative Care*, *22*(1), 161. https://doi.org/10.1186/s12904-023-01286-2

Lewis, C. S. (2001). *The problem of pain*. HarperSanFrancisco.

Mace, N. L., & Rabins, P. V. (2011). *The 36-hour day: A family guide to caring for people who have Alzheimer disease, related dementias, and memory loss* (5th ed). Johns Hopkins University Press.

Miller, M. (2020, March 6). *How to evaluate an alzheimer's memory care program five star senior living*. Five Star Senior Living. https://www.fivestarseniorliving.com/blog/how-to-evaluate-an-alzheimers-memory-care-program

Opfell, O. S. (1982). *The king james bible translators*. McFarland.

Peck, M. S. (1978). *The road less traveled: A new psychology of love, traditional values, and spiritual growth*. Simon and Schuster.

Peterson, E. H. (Ed.). (2002). *The Message: The Bible in contemporary language*. NavPress.

Practical solutions for caregiver stress. (n.d.). Mayo Clinic. Retrieved May 6, 2024, from https://www.mayoclinic.org/healthy-lifestyle/stress-management/in-depth/caregiver-stress/art-20044784

Seniorly. (n.d.). *21 highly rated apps for family caregivers*. Seniorly Inc. Retrieved March 25, 2024, from https://www.seniorly.com/resource-center/caregivers/10-helpful-caregiver-apps

Setting routines and reminders. (n.d.). Alzheimer Society of Canada. Retrieved April 13, 2024, from https://alzheimer.ca/en/help-support/im-caring-person-living-dementia/providing-day-day-care/setting-routines-reminders

Smith, P. D., Martin, B., Chewning, B., Hafez, S., Leege, E., Renken, J., & Ramos, R. S. (2018). Improving healthcare communication for caregivers: A pilot study. *Gerontology & Geriatrics Education*, *39*(4), 433–444. https://doi.org/10.1080/02701960.2016.1188810

Stories from a Caregiver. (n.d.). *Meaning and Hope Institute*. Retrieved March 21, 2024, from https://meaningandhope.org/stories-from-a-caregiver/

Studies show benefits of caregiver support programs. (2015, June 2). National Institutes of Health (NIH). https://www.nih.gov/news-events/nih-research-matters/studies-show-benefits-caregiver-support-programs

Taking a person with alzheimer's disease to the hospital. (2024, July 8). National Institute on Aging. https://www.nia.nih.gov/health/alzheimers-caregiving/taking-person-alzheimers-disease-hospital

ten Bosch, Brenda. (2024). *Wall Pilates for Seniors Made Easy: A 28 Day Step by Step Guide Toward Greater Functional Strength, Enhanced Stability, and Increased Vitality using Illustrated Exercises*. Self-Published.

The new age of alzheimer's. (n.d.). Scientific American. https://www.scientificamerican.com/custom-media/the-new-age-of-alzheimers/

Towns, E. L. (2008). *Stewardship: Learning to Manage Your Life* .

Upenieks, L. (2023). Unpacking the relationship between prayer and anxiety: A consideration of prayer types and expectations in the united states. *Journal of Religion and Health, 62*(3), 1810–1831. https://doi.org/10.1007/s10943-022-01708-0

Van der Kolk, B. A. (2015). *The body keeps the score: Brain, mind and body in the healing of trauma.* Penguin Books.

Warren, R. (2002). *The purpose-driven life: What on earth am I here for?* Zondervan.

What equipment can improve the home of a person with dementia? | Alzheimer's Society. (n.d.). Retrieved April 16, 2024, from https://www.alzheimers.org.uk/get-support/staying-independent/what-equipment-improve-adapt-home-person-dementia

What is dementia? Symptoms, types, and diagnosis. (2022, December 8). National Institute on Aging. https://www.nia.nih.gov/health/alzheimers-and-dementia/what-dementia-symptoms-types-and-diagnosis

Made in the USA
Coppell, TX
20 December 2024

43211196R00134